Katherine
PATERSON

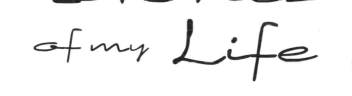

Stories of my Life

Dial Books for Young Readers
an imprint of Penguin Group (USA) LLC

DIAL BOOKS FOR YOUNG READERS
Published by the Penguin Group
Penguin Group (USA) LLC
375 Hudson Street, New York, New York 10014

USA / Canada / UK / Ireland / Australia / New Zealand / India / South Africa / China
penguin.com
A Penguin Random House Company

Library of Congress Cataloging-in-Publication Data
Paterson, Katherine.
Stories of my life / Katherine Paterson.
pages cm
ISBN 978-0-8037-4043-3 (hardcover)
1. Paterson, Katherine. 2. Authors, American—20th century—Biography.
3. Children's stories—Authorship. I. Title.
PS3566.A779Z46 2014 813'.54—dc23 [B]

Printed in the United States of America
1 3 5 7 9 10 8 6 4 2

Designed by Nancy R. Leo-Kelly
Text set in ITC Galliard

These stories are for my children,
Lin, John Jr., David, and Mary,
and their "little sister," Mary Cecile,
also
for my grandchildren,
Katherine, Margaret, Carter, Griffin, Decker, Jordan, Liam,
plus Katie,
and as always, for John

Table of Contents

A Few Words from Kate DiCamillo

I don't remember when Katherine first told me about Maud Henderson and Robert E. Lee and the last kiss. I only know that the story delighted me so much that I kept asking Katherine to tell it to me again.

At some point, I asked her to write the story down.

Actually, I threatened her.

I told her that if she didn't write the story, I would do it.

I didn't mean it. Not really. I just wanted to know more about Maud.

Happily, Maud's story is in this book. The last kiss is in this book. General Robert E. Lee's horse, Traveller, is in this book, and the bones of Traveller are here as well.

This is the story of a life.

It is the story of a first-grade girl who did not receive any valentines. That first grader grew up to be a writer, and when the writer's mother asked her why she hadn't written about that terrible day of no valentines, the writer answered her by saying, "All my books are about the day I didn't get any valentines."

This book is a valentine.

It is Katherine's valentine to her parents and to her children. It is her valentine to life and to stories.

It is her valentine to us.

And even though the stories are written down, I love them so much that I might still ask for Katherine to tell them to me again.

My Friend Katherine
by Nancy Price Graff

For almost fifteen years Katherine and I have had lunch together weekly. For eight of those years we have eaten at a diner midway between our Vermont homes and across the highway from the state garage. The diner is a family operation, clean, efficient, and democratic, but our loyalty has earned us the equivalent of frequent flyer status. We get priority seating. We have a designated waitress, Charlotte, who sometimes has Katherine's water and my iced tea on the table even before we reach our booth. Our immutable order—BLTs and lemon meringue pie—arrives promptly. We can stay for one hour or two. At some point Charlotte decides Katherine has had enough and switches her to decaf. But this isn't why I come.

I come for the conversation, which, in a word, is extraordinary. More often than not, we start talking even before we shrug out of our coats and slide into one of the green booths. Katherine plants both hands on the table, palms down, and leans forward. Her eyes sparkle with mischief. She can no more contain the story welling within her than she can stifle a sneeze.

Week after week, one of the greatest storytellers in the world has told me the story of her exceptional life. Diners no more than three feet away, deep into their meatloaf, are oblivious to the presence of the former National Ambassador for Young People's Literature, the winner of the Astrid Lindgren Award and the Hans Christian Andersen Medal. It would never cross their minds that the gray-haired woman sitting two booths over, wearing a turtleneck and a pink sweater, might have had dinner last week with the Librarian of Congress or the empress of Japan.

Week after week, as Katherine nibbles at her sandwich, stories billow from her as if they were smoke and she were a furnace on the coldest day of the year. It seems, at times, as if she has lived a dozen lives, not just the one I know. Over the years I've discerned a pattern of before and afters: before she left China and after, before she left for college and after, before she met John and after, before she had children and after, before she started to write and after. At one lunch Katherine said she didn't really care about the fame that has found her. I challenged her. "You enjoy the fame," I said. "Look at the opportunities it has brought you that you never imagined having." She smiled sheepishly. So there is also before and after she realized that she could make a difference.

Katherine rarely speaks of the book she is working on. Still, the air between us fills with chatter. Hands wave in the air. There are regular bursts of laughter. We talk about our lives, our families, the books we're reading, our travel, our disappointments, politics, world events, and whether we will continue writing. For her, it never gets any easier. She has written more than thirty books in forty years, but each time she finishes a book, she worries that she will never again feel the inspiration of another story rising in her. I have heard this more than once.

But I don't worry. Over the course of our friendship, I have seen Katherine whoop with laughter and I have seen her cry. I have seen her playful, sad, wistful, tired, thoughtful, and most often hopeful and happy, which seems to be her natural disposition. But I have never seen her speechless. Every week there are more stories. Many in this collection I've never heard before, and others I've heard more than once, but every story in the hands of a great storyteller finds new life with every telling. These stories hint at how Katherine performs what she calls the "fragile magic" of spinning her stories for children and young adults, but anyone who reads enough of them will find the wellspring of the waters that have nourished this woman's remarkable life.

INTRODUCTION

My daughter Lin was very ill when she was pregnant with her first child, and I went to try to help out. It was hard to know how to take care of her. She could keep virtually nothing in her stomach and most of the time simply lay in a dark room feeling miserable. I soon ran out of topics for conversation, until one day I remembered a story my mother had told me, so I said: "Surely I told you about the time . . ." But I hadn't. She'd never heard the story I'd grown up knowing. I couldn't believe I'd never told it to her, just as my mother had told it to me. And then I realized what had happened. I heard most of those stories at the kitchen sink while Mother was washing and my sister Liz and I were drying and putting away the dishes. For most of my children's lives, we'd had a dishwasher.

I resolved then that I would write down the kitchen sink stories of my family, and write about my own life for my children and grandchildren and the several friends who thought I should write more about my childhood. But as I wrote and people began to read it, I added more and more. The thing just got out of hand and grew, not into a proper memoir, but beyond the simple collection of stories I'd first intended. Since writing a memoir has become all the rage, I found I could hardly give a talk without someone asking when I was going to write my memoirs. Well, call it ego or whatever you like, I decided if I was going to write the stories for my family and friends, I might just as well make them into a proper book with a proper editor and publisher instead of just doing them privately. I am a writer, after all, and I do love to tell stories—the bigger the audience, the better.

I've filled out details in the anecdotal tales about my parents with letters and brief memoirs that my parents wrote down when they were the age I am now. I'd taken a tape recorder to their house and asked them to talk their remembrances into it, but they were put off by the technology and decided instead to write them down for us five children. My father's time in the Washington and Lee Ambulance Corps was augmented by the memoirs of a fellow driver, William Roth.

My mother's mother had saved her letters from China, but they were less than satisfying. Much of the writing was intent on not worrying her mother when, in truth, her life in China was filled with many anxious times. After my father died, I remarked to his surviving sisters that it was a pity he had written so few letters, as I guessed his might have told more about our lives there. "What do you mean?" one of my old aunts asked. "He wrote Mama every week."

"I don't guess you still have those letters," I said, not daring to hope.

She looked at me with disgust. "Well, we wouldn't have thrown them away." A few weeks later they came to my house in an old cardboard box—not every letter he wrote, I feel sure, but many more than I could have ever hoped for, starting with a few from his time in the army through the years 1923–1940, which were spent in China.

The longest story in the book is not exactly a family story, though the germ of it was told to me both by my parents and Maud Henderson herself. My friend and fellow writer Kate DiCamillo heard the short version and told me that if I didn't write about Maud, she would, which drove me to research Maud's life. To my surprised delight, I discovered that her letters from China to her half sister and a few others had been given to the library at the University of North Carolina. There were also records and letters in the historical archives of the Episcopal Church and references to Maud in the memoirs of Marian Craighill, the wife of an Episcopal bishop in China.

I am indebted to all these sources, but especially to my mother, who told me stories at the kitchen sink.

Stories
of my Life

Photo taken by Jill Paton Walsh that I used for publicity until I got teased about aging when the photo hadn't.

Three Frequently Asked Questions

Question #1: How did you become a writer?

When I'm asked this question, I usually ask the questioner if he would like to hear my first published work. If he looks at all interested I proceed to recite:

> Pat, pat, pat.
> There is the rat.
> Where is the cat?
> Pat, pat, pat.

This piece appeared in the Shanghai American School newspaper in the fall of 1939. Right beside it was a letter from my teacher, Miss Essie Shields, that began: "The second graders' work is not up to our usual standards this week . . ." ensuring that my first published work would be forever linked to my first critical review.

Hardly anything has survived of my childhood writing. I can't remember that there was very much to begin with. I was a reader, not a writer. I do have one letter that I wrote the same year as "Pat Pat Pat." My parents went to China as Presbyterian missionaries in 1923. The war between China and Japan began in 1937, and in 1939 my mother and we five children spent the year in Shanghai, while my father went back to our hometown of Huai'an, which was under Japanese occupation. The trip was determined to be too dangerous for family travel, as it required the crossing and re-crossing of battle lines and bandit country. Even though we were never sure that mail would get through when he was "up country," we would write to him. Once, trying to be very grown-up, I thought I'd imitate the way my mother often closed her letters, which was "Lovingly, Mary." My older brother and sister saw my letter and hooted. Not ever having been a strong speller, I'd signed it: "Lovely, Katherine," a misspelling I was often reminded of through the years. But somehow, despite the chaotic times, my letter reached my father and, amazing as it seems to me, he kept it. When I found it and reread it years later, I was pleased to see that although at school

I was imitating my hated Dick and Jane primers, when I wrote to my father, whose love I trusted, I could write pretty well for a second grader.

The truth is that, even though I was a very early reader (which made me hate the school texts, which bore no resemblance in my mind to real books), no one thought I had the makings of a writer, including me. I couldn't decide whether I wanted to be a missionary or a movie star when I grew up.

My writing life almost didn't happen. During my last year at the Presbyterian School of Christian Education in Richmond, Virginia, one of my favorite professors stopped me in the hall and said she'd just been reading my exam and it made her wonder if I'd ever thought of becoming a writer. Now, I, the lifelong reader, the summa cum laude graduate in English literature, knew what great writing was, so how could Dr. Little imagine, on the basis of an essay on an exam, that I should be a writer? "No," I said primly, I had no intention of being a writer because "I wouldn't want to add another mediocre writer to the world."

"Maybe," Dr. Little said, "that's what God is calling you to be."

It was hard for me to imagine that God needed a lot more mediocre writers in the world, so I didn't become a writer or a movie star, I became a missionary. It took me a long time to understand what Sara Little was really saying, and it was this: There are no guarantees of success, much less of quality. If you don't dare to be a mediocre writer, you'll never be a writer at all.

In the end, it was Sara Little who set me firmly on the journey.

She recommended me for the scholarship at Union Seminary, where I met John Paterson, a young Presbyterian pastor from Buffalo, New York. I married him the following summer, and didn't return to my life as a missionary. So then she suggested to the Board of Christian Education that I be asked to write a book on the Christian faith for fifth and sixth graders.

I began to write *Who Am I?* at about the time our first son, John Jr., was born, and it was published in 1966 after Lin had arrived and David was born. I realized that I loved to write and that I wasn't going back to teaching with three tiny ones around, so I began to write in earnest. I needed something in those days that wasn't, by the end of the day, eaten up, torn up, or dirtied up. I needed something to keep my mind from turning into mush. And so I began to write in what snatches of time I could find when all three children were safely asleep and my minister husband was off visiting the sick and comforting the dying. My desk was the dining room table that had to be cleaned off before we could use it for any other purpose. That I didn't always perform this task in time is proven by childish scribblings on pages of the first draft of *The Sign of the Chrysanthemum.*

I didn't start with a novel. I didn't know where to start. I tried poetry, essays, short stories, none of which anyone wanted to buy. A woman in the Takoma Park church knew I was trying to write. She asked if I'd like to go with her to a writing course being offered through the county adult education program. I was thrilled with the idea. Mom's night out! We took the general writing course and then, when a course in writing for children was offered, we took that as well.

I got two valuable lessons from those courses. The first was that to be a writer you have to write. I have always been a student who does her homework, and I was embarrassed to go to a weekly class unprepared. So I was writing, sometimes in five-minute snatches of time, but writing something almost every day. Even after I no longer had the framework of the class, I knew that I needed to keep working in a disciplined fashion or I'd never finish anything. The second lesson I learned seems to contradict the first—it is that I did not again want to be a part of a writing group. I don't like to share early drafts for several people to read and comment on. Other writers I know and admire swear by their writers' groups, but I learned fairly early on that I am not that kind of writer. I'm a very private person. I need to do my work with no one reading over my shoulder or a group of people discussing it, even a supportive group.

Seven years elapsed between the publication of *Who Am I?* and the publication of *The Sign of the Chrysanthemum*—seven years during which I was writing regularly and trying to sell what I had written. I sold one short story to a tiny magazine that ceased publication the month after it printed my story. I also sold one poem, but the magazine that paid ten dollars for it died before the poem was ever published.

I decided that since I was writing a story or a poem almost every week I would try to write, instead, a chapter every week, so that by the end of the year, I'd have a book, and even if no one ever published it, it would be something substantial that I had accomplished.

Question #2: Where do you get your ideas?

Some of my writer friends have so many ideas, they'll never live long enough to turn them all into books. I look at them with a certain envy, for when I finish a book I say, "Well, that was a great career while it lasted," because I am sure I'll never have an idea worthy of another book. But by now I've written a lot of books, so I must have gotten those ideas from somewhere, and that somewhere is most often from my own life. Another lesson I've learned along the way is that there are no truly original ideas. There are no truly original plots. As the writer of the book of Ecclesiastes said three thousand or so years ago: "There is no new thing under the sun." Except you. Except me. Every individual is new and unique, so we may be stuck with the same old plots, but because a new person is telling the story, bringing his or her singular life to bear on the story, it is fresh and new. So the only excuse I have for daring to write is that no one else in the world would be able to tell the stories that only I can tell. And an aside to those of you wishing to write—that is your excuse as well. The raw material for our unique stories is our unique lives and perspective on life.

I have a note card that has lived for years in my desk drawer.

The card has three panel illustrations. At the top lies a zonked-out whale with *X*'s where its eyes should be. Below is the same beached whale with its eyes popped wide open in amazement as a voice coming from its mouth declares: "Incredible as it seems—" The sentence is completed by a person emerging from between the jaws of the beast: "—my life is based on a true story." This book contains true stories of my life that I want to share with people I care about, a lot of whom are readers of my books. Sometimes a reader, often a friend, when hearing me tell an old story, will recognize in the story the seed of one of my books that I myself hadn't realized. That's one of the great things about having readers. They often know more than the writer.

This book is not a memoir. I swore never to write one. My memory is not good enough to turn these stories into a coherent narrative. Besides, I can't believe the people I love would want to be minor characters in the story of my life. I've gotten permission from my husband and children to tell tales on them, but I'm hesitant to impose on others. So there will be many important people in my life that will not appear as characters in these stories. You know who you are. If you're relieved, good; if you're disappointed, I apologize.

Question #3: "How does it feel to be famous?"

The questioner is young and earnest and has just confided that although she doesn't know what she wants to be, she knows she wants to be famous. I don't really know how to answer her question. How *does* it feel to be famous?

And then I remember things that happened after *Bridge to Terabithia* won the Newbery Medal. I would be invited somewhere to speak and there would be a lovely dinner at which I was the honored guest. The people on either side of me at the table would say something gracious and congratulatory and then they would turn to the person on the other side and never speak to me again for the whole meal. There were a few times when the person in charge made it clear that she'd hired me for the weekend and expected to get her money's worth, by gum.

I'd come home and whine to my long-suffering husband. "I'm a human being," I'd say, "why can't they just treat me like a human being."

And then I remembered Anita. When I was in Chandler Junior High in Richmond, Virginia, all of us new kids were put in the same homeroom. It was a wonderful thing because we could make friends with each other, we didn't have to try to cope with already cemented cliques that populated the rest of the school. I made several good friends that year, but there was one new girl that we were all shy around. The reason we were shy around Anita was because she was famous. She was the youngest member of the Carter sisters. Her mother, Maybelle, had been part of the legendary country music group the Carter Family. Her older sister June went on to marry Johnny Cash. At the time, her mother, two older sisters, and Anita sang regularly on the radio, and in concerts all over the South. We didn't make friends with her because we didn't know what to say to someone we considered famous.

Because she had moved around the country a lot, Anita needed catching up in a couple of subjects and for some reason I was asked to tutor her. To my amazement she was so shy that even one on one, she barely spoke above a whisper. Yet that summer I went to a concert at the stadium, and on stage, Anita was transformed. The huge crowd loved her and she obviously loved performing for them.

"If it is hard for me at forty-five to deal with the little bit of fame that I have, how must it have been for Anita?" I wondered. So I wrote *Come Sing, Jimmy Jo* about James, a shy boy who becomes a star. If you want to know what Katherine Paterson is really like, you should read that book. Like James, and perhaps Anita, I'm a shy show-off—a very private person who loves to perform.

When my friend Nancy Graff read this section on feeling famous she said, "Oh, c'mon, Katherine, you know you get a kick out of being famous." We both laughed. I mean, I was thrilled to be introduced to the empress of Japan and hear her say, "Katherine Paterson? Who wrote *Bridge to Terabithia*?" Sometimes I can't believe my own life. I find myself standing on a stage or sitting at a table with writers I have known and admired for many years—really famous people— and think: "This is *me* here with these amazing people." I want to give myself the proverbial pinch to make sure I'm awake.

But that doesn't mean I *feel* famous. Famous is not an emotion like love or hate or jealousy or fear—feelings with which I am well acquainted. You can't feel it, but you can learn over the years to sit back and enjoy the perks.

Autographing grandson Decker Paterson's book at the Library of Congress ceremony 2010.

When *The Master Puppeteer* won the National Book Award in 1977, all my friends in the Washington area rejoiced with me. The following year, *Bridge to Terabithia* won the Newbery Medal and they threw another big party. Fortunately, I moved in 1979 and they didn't have to give me yet another party when *The Great Gilly Hopkins* won the National Book Award and was the Newbery Honor book. By this time I was afraid I wouldn't have a single writer friend left. I was Biblical Job in reverse: "Why me, God? Why me?" And the answer seemed to be: *Now people will listen to what you say, so you'd better say something worth listening to.* When *Jacob Have I Loved* won a Newbery two years later, I tried to remember that. I also learned that my friends were among the most gracious people in the world.

My special friend in Takoma Park, Maryland, was Gene Namovicz. Gene was an established writer when I first met her, but not long after we became friends, my second novel was published, then the next four that all won national prizes. Gene stood by me in my triumphs, just as she would through my troubles, and always with a wonderful sense of humor.

Soon after the first Newbery, I was scheduled to give a speech that I knew had to be a good one, since it seemed to me that almost every important writer and critic on both sides of the Atlantic was going to be in the audience. We were on vacation at Lake George, so I sent the speech to Gene for her comments and revised accordingly. But I was still anxious. I called her and told her she'd just have to pray for me, as I was afraid I was going to fall apart. Gene, a devout Roman Catholic, promised she'd pray, but told me to calm down. It would be fine, and it was. I called her to tell her it had gone all right and thanked her for her prayers.

"If I'd known how efficacious Roman Catholic prayers were," I said, jokingly, "I might have converted long ago."

"Well, I did pray," she said, "and He said, 'Katherine who?'"

When I moved to Vermont, Gene got in touch with Grace Greene, a friend I had made soon after moving, and told her that as long as I was in Maryland and even in Virginia, she had been able to keep me humble, but Vermont was just too far away, so she was turning the job over to Grace. I wondered if Grace had taken her assignment too much to heart when she told me this story. A small group of us gather periodically to do pastel painting and the night of January 5, 2010, I was missing. Grace had gotten an invitation, so she knew that I was in Washington being presented as the new National Ambassador for Young People's Literature, but when the others asked where I was, Grace said: "She's in Washington being made a national embarrassment." When she realized what she had said, she tried to correct herself. "Oh, no, I mean *natural* embarrassment." Gene would have loved that very Freudian slip.

Since real friends like mine are more precious than awards, I know I am truly blessed, and gratitude, unlike fame, is something you can actually feel.

Anne and baby Mary Goetchius.

Mary Elizabeth Goetchius

When I'm asked about censorship, I recall that my parents, conservative Presbyterian missionaries, never censored what we children read. In fact, when I was eleven or twelve, Mother would hand me the book-of-the-month selection that she'd failed to return before the deadline and ask me to read it to see if it was worth her time. When I was eleven, she gave me a copy of *The Yearling*, a Pulitzer Prize–winning book she had read. She knew it contained profane language and "inappropriate content," but

15

she gave it to me because she knew I would love it. I did love it. Reading it as an adult I see how much that book has influenced me as a writer.

Mother was a big fan of my books and promoted them to the extent that I wondered after she died, who was going to buy them now that she was gone. When I got word that *The Great Gilly Hopkins* was the Newbery Honor book (that year for some mysterious reason there was only one), I was told that I couldn't tell anyone until after the official press conference. I decided that one's dying mother didn't count as telling and called her at once. She could barely speak by then, but when I told her the news, she asked in the playful voice I knew so well: "That naughty child?"

Mother was born in Waco, Texas, but that didn't make her a Texan. She always said that her father left Georgia and took his family to Texas to seek his fortune, but all he found was her, so they all went back to Georgia. They settled in Rome, where her father's older brother George was pastor of a Presbyterian church. She was named Mary and was the middle of her parents' three girls. Anne, the oldest, was an artist who ironically always suffered from poor eyesight. Helen, the youngest, was a bit of a rebel who often caused their straight-laced mother anxiety. But my mother was, it appears, the "good child." Grandmother referred to her as "my little missionary," pointing her at an early age toward service as a "foreign missionary." In addition to the two eldest brothers who died in the Civil War, her father had two other older brothers—George, the minister, who was elected for a term as Moderator of the General Assembly of the (then) Southern Presbyterian Church—and Henry, a prosperous lawyer, who, being childless, wanted to adopt my mother. Henry never quite forgave my grandfather for not giving up one of his daughters (after all, he had a surplus) and at length adopted a son who inherited his entire estate.

Mother never minded being the daughter of a respectable, but certainly not wealthy, insurance and real estate salesman. As a child I often begged for stories of the "olden days," when she was young. (My own children, referring to *my* youth, would say: "Back when you were alive, Mom . . ."—protests that I was still alive notwithstanding.) Mother always spoke with delight about growing up on Third Avenue in Rome, Georgia. Everyone seemed to live across the street from the Goetchius family. There was Uncle George and after his death in 1900, the new Presbyterian pastor, Dr. Sydnor, and his family with children roughly the same age as the Goetchius girls. Woodrow Wilson's first wife grew up there, and Mother remembered her father, an elder in the Presbyterian church, acting as a pall bearer when Mrs. Wilson was brought back to Rome to be buried. There was, supposedly, a thank-you note from the president that never surfaced—much like the many Abraham Lincoln letters floating around that lived on in some family's legend but not in its archives.

I was most envious of the neighborhood group of eight or

nine girls just her age. Mother was an active member of the Third Avenue Gang, who had "spend-the-night parties," progressive dinners, went to baseball games; in short, did everything together. One of the girls had a dollhouse in her backyard that became the gang's clubhouse and the center of their activities until well up into their teens. When she talked about her childhood friends I was always envious. The idea of living in the same house for all your childhood and having the same knot of devoted friends seemed magical to me, who had lived in thirteen different places by the time I was thirteen. Years later, she went back to Rome for a reunion of the Third Avenue Gang, one of whom had married an heir of one of the early Hawaiian missionary families and another whose son wrote racy novels that had Rome in a twitter.

Summers as children we would go to the farm in Virginia where our spinster aunts and bachelor uncles were strict maintainers of good behavior, but the Goetchius girls would go to Eufala, Alabama, to visit their beloved aunt Anne or aunt Annie, as they called her. (I grew up thinking her name was "Aunt Tanny.") She was Grandmother's older and only sibling. As children, one of our witticisms was "Eufala? I picka you up." Annie lived on a farm and produced six children and a brood of descendents, most of whom my generation never met. The exception was Cousin Wade Herren, known in the family as "Apple," since it was accepted that he was the "apple of his mother's eye." Wade became a general during World War II, and we met him when he was stationed in Washington sometime after the war. He told us proudly, not of his exploits during the war, but of how honored he was to be the military escort for Princess Elizabeth on her official visit to Washington not too long before she became the Queen of England. "Beautiful manners. Just like a lovely young Southern girl," he enthused.

The Goetchius girls loved the farm with their many cousins and all the African American field and house help there. On the Herren farm the children could run barefoot and take the pony cart out to the field and fill it with watermelons, hoping, perhaps encouraging, one to roll off and burst so that they could sit down and eat it in the middle of the path.

My grandmother Elizabeth Gertrude Daniel Goetchius was known as "Trudy" when she was a child, a playful nickname that seemed totally unlikely to me, who only knew her as a forbidding figure. I always called her "Grandmother Goetchius" or at least "Grandmother," never Granny or Grandma or Nana or any of the diminutives by which my friends spoke fondly of their grandmothers.

I never knew my grandfather Charlie Goetchius, and it is one of the sorrows of my life. In his picture—I've only seen one— he's a man I know I would have loved. He had red hair and a bushy mustache to match. I think I can see a mischievous light in his eyes, even in a formal photograph. Aunt Helen told me that she was "his girl," and I believed her because I imagined he would have admired, not feared, that rebellious streak in his youngest daughter. An adventurous man of sorts, he was one of the first people in Rome to buy an automobile. Since Anne's eyesight was poor, and Helen was too young, he decided to teach his daughter Mary how to drive. The lessons ceased abruptly when Mother drove his new Ford through the plate glass window of the local drugstore. Though only the window and the auto suffered damage, she didn't take up driving again until she was in her fifties, when she and I took driving lessons from the same instructor after my father had given up on both of us. Ironically, it was Anne who soon afterward became an expert driver and was the first young woman in North Georgia to drive in parades and funerals.

Just before Anne was set to go to college, a relative came to be president of Shorter College, a half-hour walk from their Third Avenue home. After graduating, Anne went off to art school in Boston. Mother was barely sixteen when she entered Shorter, where she studied biology, having decided that she wanted to be a doctor. Doctors were badly needed in China, which she seemed to have decided early on would be the place to spend her life. Then during her senior year she was summoned out of class and told that her father was dead, felled by a massive heart attack for which there had been no warning.

Not only had she lost her father, she had lost any hope of becoming a doctor. There was no money for medical school and besides, how could she leave her mother at such a time? The solution was to find a teaching position in the area. Helen was still at home, so she taught that first year in Clinton, South Carolina, but when Helen left to go to nursing school, she returned to Rome to be with her mother.

By then America was at war. Along with several of her friends, Mary worked in the Red Cross/YMCA canteen. Dressed in blue uniforms with white veils, the girls were on the platform when troop trains came through. Summer was particularly exciting because the nearby orchards would send bushels of peaches to the station. The girls stood beside each car with a bushel of peaches to hand them out when the train stopped. Mother described the "whoop of the men, mostly from the north, when they piled off the cars and saw us canteen girls presiding over the peaches. It was especially fun at night when we had flares."

Three of the girls, including Mary, loved the canteen work, and applied for an assignment overseas. They were only twenty-three and the minimum age was twenty-five, but the New York interviewer said there was a bill before Congress to lower the age, and when it passed, she would put their names at the top of the list. When the Armistice was signed in November Mother confessed to a tinge of disappointment in the midst of the rejoicing. She would not be going to France after all.

Several weeks later a wire came asking if she would be interested in an overseas assignment. Canteen workers were still needed, as the army would be in Europe for some time.

Once when we were children we were playing either Old Maids or Flinch, and I realized Mother was shuffling and bridging the deck like a riverboat gambler I'd seen in a movie. "Where did you learn how to do that?" I asked. She visibly blushed and confessed that on the boat taking her to France in 1918, she had learned to play bridge and dance—two activities her own mother would certainly have frowned on. But the chaplain in charge of the volunteers said that they would be needed skills when they arrived in France to entertain the troops.

When I was an adolescent, Mother told me about the chaplain, a kind man that all the young women liked and admired. Then one night after the dancing lesson he asked Mary to come down to his cabin for some forgotten purpose. "I was so naïve—he was the chaplain, after all—so I went. I had no idea . . ." Once there, the chaplain closed the door and threw his arms around her. Alarmed, she jammed the heel of her pump into his foot. He let go with a howl and she fled. The incident was never spoken of again until she had daughters of her own. I can remember at about thirteen staring wide-eyed at my proper mother when she thought it time to tell me this cautionary tale. I never had to utilize the heel-of-the-shoe trick myself, but I think Mother would be gratified to see that I passed it on to Lyddie Worthen for her use against her lecherous floor boss at the Lowell mill in my novel *Lyddie*.

Mother remembered her time in France as fun. The war was over and the troops were mostly on vacation. I can only assume she put her card-playing and dancing skills to use and had no more occasions on which to employ her foot-stabbing technique.

She had learned in Clinton and in Rome that she did not want to be a teacher, so on her return was delighted to take a job as a

YWCA secretary in Petersburg, Virginia, which was near a large army post. But she couldn't forget that she had planned for most of her life that she would be a missionary. She went over to Richmond, where there was a Presbyterian seminary and a new school for training women for church work, as the seminary did not enroll women in 1921. The president of the General Assembly's Training School for Lay Workers (as it was then called) was a friend of her uncle George's, and he advised her to go to Greensboro, North Carolina, to a church that had recently lost its Director of Christian Education.

She had hardly settled in Greensboro, when Dr. Edgert Smith, head of the denomination's foreign mission board and a friend of her father's, came to visit the church. The first thing he said to Mother was: "Where is Charlie Goetchius's daughter who was going to China?" "I'm the one," she said. "Well, daughter," he said, "you're not getting any younger."

Dr. Smith not only got her released from her new job, but he persuaded the church to give her a scholarship to the Assembly's Training School.

And that was where she met my father, which is the beginning of our family story.

Children in the same family have different parents. And even the same child will seem to have a different parent at a different stage in his or her life. After I was grown, my mother and I often tangled. We had a running controversy about clothes. She was very unhappy that I would not buy her grandchildren "Sunday clothes." My argument was that we couldn't possibly afford fancy clothes that could only be worn on Sundays and then not even every Sunday, clothes that would be quickly outgrown and might or might not fit a younger sibling. During the early seventies, I shocked her when she realized I, a minister's wife, wore pants around the house. "Suppose one of the women from the church should come by and see you," she said. She couldn't believe when I retorted that at our church in Takoma Park, Maryland, a number of those lovely church ladies were wearing polyester pantsuits to church services. She was hurt and puzzled when my husband joined African Americans marching for the right to vote in Alabama and spent several nights in the Selma jail. "That's not the Alabama I know," she said. And until tapes revealed that President Nixon was a world-class cusser, she defended him against all my charges. But there is a great deal of my mother in Susan Bradshaw, Louise and Caroline's mother in *Jacob Have I Loved*. It is no accident that I was writing the book while my mother was dying. The pivotal scene where Louise confronts her mother and her mother's word allows her to leave both the island and her lifelong envy of Caroline could not have been written if I had had a different mother.

One story to prove my point. I was nine years old and we had recently moved to Winston-Salem, North Carolina, where my father had been called to serve on the staff of the First Presbyterian Church and to begin a new congregation in a community just out from town. The church had found us a house and furnished it, and we had frequent visits from members. On these occasions Mother would always serve a rather elaborate Chinese tea. The pièce de la résistance of these teas was her antique *denshin* box. It was a wooden box about fourteen inches square with nine beautiful porcelain interior sections. In each of the separate sections Mother would put a different treat—sunflower seeds, pumpkin seeds, watermelon seeds, sesame cookies, and peanuts. Usually small Western cookies or candies would com-

This picture appeared in the Winston-Salem Journal and Sentinel in the fall of 1941 when we had just moved there. The famous denshin box is on the table.

plete the nine sections and keep the refreshments from seeming too exotic.

One particular afternoon I had decided to be helpful. The *denshin* box needed to be refilled. I carried it carefully to the kitchen and filled each lovely little section. Then, just as I started back toward the living room, the heavy kitchen door swung back, and the box and all its contents went crashing to the floor. Mother's precious antique sections lay in several dozen pieces at my feet.

Before I could even start to cry, my mother was at the door. She didn't even glance at the floor. She looked straight into my stricken face. "Are you all right, darling?" she asked. At that point I burst into tears, but she put her arm around me and told me not to worry. Daddy could probably glue the thing back together anyhow. I was nine, but I knew that day that as long as I lived I would remember that my mother had cared more about how her child felt than any cherished antique, and I resolved that if I ever had any children I would remember that scene. I must never forget that a child's feelings are always more important than any possession.

The Lexington farm house.

George Raymond Womeldorf

When we were reading submissions for the National Book Award, Julius Lester, who was also on the jury, said wistfully that he wished we could see at least one book that had a good father in it. Soon after that I began to write *Preacher's Boy* because I knew what it meant to have a good father. Robbie's father in the book is a minister who loves his children wisely and well. My minister father sprang from stern Calvinist roots, and I, being a whiney, attention-craving child, often disappointed him. But I know he loved his children every bit as much as Robbie's father did, and one day when I was fourteen, I understood that fact in a way I never had before.

World War II ended the summer of 1945, and the following summer we prepared to return to China. My parents had spent nearly eighteen years as missionaries there, and my father, especially, could hardly wait to return. I think all of us were eager to go home at last. My father had given up his work in Winston-Salem. We suffered through all the needed shots, including the inoculation for black plague. We had made the rounds of the relatives to say good-bye for another seven years, when the word came down from the mission board that the inflation rate was through the roof in China and our departure would be delayed. We had no home to go back to, but someone lent us an unheated summer cottage in the mountains for a few months until an apartment in the complex for missionaries in Richmond, Virginia, opened up in the late fall.

My father was hardly ever there. The mission board had him traveling all over the South speaking in churches and to college groups about missions. The idea was that at any time the mission board would give us the go-ahead to go back to China. By now my brother Ray was in training to become a navy pilot and my sister Elizabeth was ready to go to college, so they would not be going with the family. But my two younger sisters, Helen and Anne, and I were scheduled to return with our parents.

There was a large desk in the Richmond apartment that was,

quite naturally, my father's workspace. In a big family it is important for individual privacy to be respected. We did not go into each other's bureau drawers, much less into Daddy's desk. But I was desperate for paper that I needed for a school project and went into his desk hoping to find some. What I found instead was an official-looking letter from the mission board. If I had no business going into his desk, I certainly had no right at all to read his mail, but the envelope had long ago been opened and I was curious. I pulled the letter out and read it. Several months before, the executive had written to say that given the current rate of inflation, sending Katherine to high school in Shanghai would be too expensive that if my folks would leave me behind, they could return to China at any time.

I can still feel the tremor that went through my body. My father's closest friends were Chinese, as well as the life's work he believed God had called him to do. China was home and we longed to go home. We could not and *it was all my fault.* If it weren't for me, my parents and younger sisters would be back in China already. Other missionary parents were leaving their children behind. In the apartment across the hall, Margaret, who was just my age, was going to be left with friends in Richmond while her parents returned to Korea.

I don't know how many days it was before my father came back from his trip. It seemed like years. When he finally returned, I had to first confess that I had gone into his desk, worse, that I had read a letter addressed to him, and then I had to say that I knew

29

why we hadn't left for China yet. I somehow stumbled through all those confessions, and then I said, as bravely as I could manage, "I know how much you want to go. It's all right if you go without me."

Daddy looked at me with the most loving expression I had ever seen. "Sweet girlie," he said, using his pet name for his four daughters. "Sweet girlie, we wouldn't leave you behind."

In the Book of Genesis, Abraham believes that God is commanding him to sacrifice his beloved son as proof of his love and obedience. But just as Abraham is about to thrust the knife into his terrified child, an angel grasps his hand and there in the thicket is a sheep that God has provided for the sacrifice. Most people find this story horrifying, but what my father taught me that day was this: No matter how sacred the calling appears, it is not God's will for parents to sacrifice their children.

It is no secret that my books have often been attacked by Conservative Christians, people whose core theology would probably be quite close to my father's. One such person, who was very critical of the language Gilly uses in *The Great Gilly Hopkins*, asked me testily, "What would your *father* think of such a book?" And I was happy to reply that of all my books published before his death, *The Great Gilly Hopkins* was his favorite. "Of course," I added with a bit of the mischievous spirit I inherited from him, "my father had read Jesus' parable of *The Prodigal Son*."

George Raymond Womeldorf, whom I called Daddy until the day he died, claimed that the only whipping he ever got was in the Sunnyside one-room schoolhouse. It seems that every school day closed with the Lord's Prayer and during the middle of the prayer one evening, the boy behind him hit him in the back, and Raymond (as he was always called at home, since his father was George) came out with a "strange noise." The elderly teacher, Mr. Hall Lackey, whipped both boys but not, according to Daddy, very severely.

My father was born on a farm a few miles out of Lexington, Virginia, on September 7, 1893 (or 1894; the records disagree.) His parents were George William Womeldorf and Lillie Belle Clements. He started at Sunnyside School at the age of five with his older brother, William, and his two older sisters, Katherine and Mamie. Maude, Joshua, Herman, Cora Belle, and Florence came along in due time. He characterized himself as something of a runt who didn't start growing until his early teens and was consequently able to slip along between the ends of the double desks and the wall and visit his friends without being seen by the teacher. There were five-year-olds and twenty-five-year-olds among the thirty-plus students, though the older boys only came to school when the weather was too bad to work on their family farms.

Except for the bullying of the small boys by the larger ones, he remembered his school days at Sunnyside as pleasant ones. Everyone had to work to keep the building going. The boys chopped wood and carried water, which was a coveted task, for the boys enjoyed the leisurely stroll to the spring. The girls, sometimes with help from the boys, swept the floor. He wondered how anyone learned anything at Sunnyside with all the different ages and stages of students. No grades were given, and the learning was a bit haphazard. This may help explain why my father was twenty when he enrolled in Washington and Lee University even though he started elementary school when he was not quite six.

At some point, Mr. Lackey retired and a Miss Ella Pultz took over. The lady was very strict and an excellent teacher. At some point she closed the building at Sunnyside and moved the school to her home, which was a three-mile trek each way from the Womeldorf farm, but Raymond recalled that "the deeper the snow, the better we liked it."

When William and Katherine were old enough to leave Miss Pultz's school, they began the seven-mile trek by foot over muddy roads to continue their education in the town of Lexington. After a year of this my grandfather decided that he needed to move closer to town. He had nine children and he wanted all of them to have a good education. It was then that he bought the farm one mile east of Lexington that I pictured as the setting for the farm in my book *Park's Quest*. The stone part of the house dated to Revolutionary War times, but most of the house was frame, Victorian style, with a gabled round window in the attic that I called a cupola in the book. The old frame barns and fields were just as I described them there, and the springhouse, which plays such an important part in the plot, was my favorite place on the farm and is depicted exactly as I remember it. I knew that one day the farm would likely pass out of the family, so I thought I could keep it if I put it into a book. Indeed, after Daddy's sisters Cora B. and Florence died, we had to sell the farm. We were sad to do so, but there were debts that had to be paid, and none of the next generation was going to be farming.

The farmhouse was on the side of a hill, and the spring that provided water and the springhouse that provided refrigeration were many feet below at the bottom of the hill. For every meal, the milk, butter, and buttermilk had to be carried up to the house and leftovers returned afterward. Water for drinking, cooking, washing, and bathing also had to be carried up the hill. It was a great day in the Womeldorf household when their forward-thinking father bought a ram, an invention that, using gravity, pumped water up to the house. The farm seems to have been a wonderful place to grow up. There were sleigh rides in the winter and, in the summer, so many peaches that they left the farm by the wagonload. And what didn't go out by wagon was peddled by the children. One of my favorite memories of the farm was the hand-cranked ice cream using the rich cream from the cows, and peaches from the orchard. The milk was so rich, in fact, that it caused my grandmother's butter to lose a blue ribbon at the fair. The judges thought she must have added coloring to make it that yellow. My Calvinist grandmother was incensed to have her integrity so impugned.

My father's high school years were spent at the Ann Smith Academy, where the principal was a scholarly gentleman by the name of Harrington Waddell, whom my father greatly admired.

This was despite the fact that Mr. Waddell gave him his only demerit. It seems a certain Billy Cox, who sat behind him in class, had stuck a needle between the sole and upper part of his shoe, and he used his homemade weapon to give Raymond a jab in his nether regions. Raymond jumped to his feet ready to give Billy a blow to the jaw when Mr. Waddell walked into the classroom.

There had been four Williams in his older brother's high school class, so all of them took the names of Caesar's generals. His brother was dubbed Titus Labienus, shortened to Labby, a nickname my father inherited when he entered the academy and which followed him through college and into the army. No other memories of high school seemed quite as vivid as the case of the lone demerit, but he did recall being in both the junior and senior class plays and was the salutatorian at graduation.

My grandparents were hardworking and devoted Presbyterians. Grandfather was an elder, and church services and Sunday school were a big part of every Sunday. They traveled by horse and buggy to the old Timber Ridge Presbyterian Church. Even after they moved closer to town, they continued to drive the eight miles back through every kind of weather. I'm not sure when they moved their membership to the church in town, but I think it was before my father left the farm for World War I.

Some of my father's earliest memories were of gathering around the piano in the parlor and singing hymns while his mother played on one of the first pianos in the area. After supper every night there were evening prayers, which consisted of Bible readings—beginning at Genesis, a chapter a night until the end of Revelation. As each of the nine children learned to read, he or she was expected to read a verse. Then they all got down on their knees while their papa prayed. This custom continued until Cora B. and Florence, the last family members, were in their nineties and unable to kneel. We grandchildren spent a lot of time on our knees trying not to giggle.

Being strong Presbyterians, every child was expected to learn both the Child's Catechism and the Westminster Shorter Catechism. So after Sunday dinner dishes were washed, the children got down to memorizing. The denomination awarded New Testaments for memorizing the Child's Catechism and Bibles for the Shorter Catechism. It didn't matter that the latter was written by the Westminster Divines in England in 1640 and adopted by the Church of Scotland in 1648; every properly brought up Presbyterian child could repeat its questions and answers by heart.

The catechism tradition lived on after my grandparents' deaths. I got my Bible in 1941, as my aunt Katherine, who was known as the champion catechism teacher in the Lexington Presbytery, was determined that her namesake be the youngest pupil she had ever coached to receive the coveted Bible. She had me follow her around the hen house while we gathered eggs. She knew all the questions by heart, of course, so she would call out: "What is God?" To which I had to immediately reply: "God is a Spirit, infinite, eternal, and unchangeable, in his being, wisdom, power, holiness, justice, goodness and truth." Or "What is sin?" To which I would cry over the clucks of the hens: "Sin is any want of conformity unto or transgression of the law of God." Neither my father nor I remembered catechism sessions as unpleasant or taxing and we were both inordinately proud of our Bibles. I still have mine with *Katherine Clements Womeldorf* embossed in gold on the worn leather cover.

The Womeldorf family loved music, and one of Daddy's happiest memories was of the day his father came home from town bearing a morning glory horn Edison phonograph with round cylinder records. "How on earth could that contraption sing and play lovely music?" he remembered marveling. The family considered it the wonder of the age and loved listening to it.

My father entered Washington and Lee University in the fall of 1913, walking the two miles from the farm every day. I once asked my father why he didn't ride a horse to school during his four years there. "I'd have to fool with the horse once I got there," he said. "It was easier just to walk." Once he took us to W and L, where we paid respects to General Lee's recumbent statue in the chapel and to the skeleton of his horse, Traveller, in the museum. My father told us that when he was in school, the skeleton of the famous horse was in the biology lab along with a skeleton of a colt. He related with great glee how student tour guides taking visitors through the buildings and grounds would point out Traveller's bones, and, then, when they got to the smaller remains, would add, "And this is Traveller as a colt." Many visitors seemed to accept this, much to the delight of the students.

While the actual Traveller bones were in the biology lab, on a day when the professor was late, the boys decided to autograph the skeleton. The ink was washed off soon afterward and the skeleton removed to the museum, but my father had signed the inside of a rib and that day we visited, he grinned mischievously and pointed out his unmistakable scrawled signature.

He entered the university the fall of 1913, and World War I began in Europe the summer after his freshman year. In 1917, at the end of his senior year, he joined the W and L ambulance corps. Training took place in Allentown, Pennsylvania. Raymond, who had never driven a car before, was placed behind the wheel of a Model T ambulance and told to drive it between two stakes. "I thought," he said, "that the point was not to knock down the stakes, so I didn't." By so doing, he had unwittingly passed his driver's test. He did plenty of marching after that day, but that single maneuver through the stakes proved to be the end of his driver education course. The next time he found himself behind the wheel was on the outskirts of Paris. "I wished many times during that drive across Paris that I'd had the sense to knock down those stakes."

G. Raymond Womeldorf's college picture.

Over There

Although my father died many years ago, a vivid reminder of his ambulance days recently arrived in a large box on my front porch. Inside was an old leather medical bag. It had come from the son of my college professor G. Parker Winship. David wrote that he had found the bag in a shop in Abingdon, Virginia, noted the unusual name, and sent it to me thinking I might know to whom it belonged. On the side in indelible ink was printed: R. G. Womeldorf, Lexington, Va, USA. The recruiter in 1917 had mis-

takenly listed my father as Raymond G. Womeldorf rather than G. Raymond—an error that caused a lot of headaches when my father applied for veteran's benefits under his correct name. What David had sent me was obviously my father's World War I medical bag. It is now in the collection at Washington and Lee.

My father never talked much about his time at the front, but I once got a glimpse of what it felt like to him. He was visiting us and we turned on Masterpiece Theater to watch *Upstairs, Downstairs,* a series to which we were somewhat addicted. The son of the household had gone to war and as the scenes of the trenches of World War I began to play on the small screen, my father stood up abruptly and left the room. I followed him out. "Is this hard for you to watch?" I asked. "Yep." It was all he said.

The Washington and Lee Ambulance Corps, also known as Section 534, landed in France on February 4, 1918. It was a month before they met the twenty adapted Model T Fords they were to drive. My father took #13 because no one else would. That next couple of weeks were spent learning how to take the engines of their "Tin Lizzies" apart and put them back together. Then the section drove from Paris to the grounds of the Palace of Versailles. The great fountains were all sandbagged; still, King Louis' palace was quite impressive to a farm boy from Virginia.

They were to be attached to the 12th French Army that had been so decimated in earlier battles that they had been withdrawn to recruit and regroup before they were once again called into action. In the meantime the 534 was ordered on March 25, 1918, to head for the front to transport wounded French soldiers from the battle of Somme. They could hardly move their vehicles forward for the stream of men, women, and children jamming the roads, desperately trying to flee the slaughter.

The job of the 534 was to evacuate stretcher cases from the dressing stations near the front to hospitals that were often simply cathedrals or warehouses. They spent two weeks doing this, never having time even to take off their clothes, much less rest. When at last they were relieved for R & R, they stopped by the US headquarters in Chaumont, where the officer in charge threatened to throw them in the brig for wearing soiled uniforms, failing to shave, and having mud on their boots. My father mused that the newly arrived Americans had never seen men from the front before. But had they known their presence would receive that kind of welcome, they would never have stopped there.

We children were brought up in a teetotaler household, but it occurred to my brother that our father might not have always been abstemious. "Daddy," he said, "when you were attached to the French army did you ever drink wine?" My father looked at him in amazement. "You don't think I would have drunk water, do you? It would have killed me."

William Roth, a teacher from Wisconsin who had been added to the W and L unit, wrote a memoir of the 534. In it he recalls an occasion when he and Labby Womeldorf went to a water fountain near the camp kitchen only to find a notice reading "eau non-potable." They filled their canteens with the dry red issue wine and, because they were so thirsty, gulped it down. Since neither of them was used to alcohol they could only make it back to their billets by holding on to the buildings along the way.

Once the two of them visited an old invalid who had been a dancer and entertainer. They took a morning glory phonograph and cylindrical records they had salvaged in the Somme and played them for the old man, who sat up in bed and beat time to the music with his arms. Around this same time they helped an elderly couple they had met by hauling in their hay and were rewarded with a lunch of bread, cheese, and wine.

Months after that Roth tells of a walk he and Labby were taking when they came upon an enormous unexploded shell with German markings on it. "Let's end it up and take our pictures beside it," said my father. While two French soldiers nearby shook their fingers and yelled "Non! Non! Non!" the crazy Americans, after a couple of tries, were able to upend the heavy shell. It stood shoulder high and, Roth guesses, weighed over a thousand pounds. Roth and Labby each took a picture of the other holding up the shell. When it didn't explode, the French soldiers came running over to have their pictures taken, but Labby shook his index finger and said "Non! Non! Non!" and tipped the shell back onto to the ground.

"It seemed," says Roth, "that Labby liked to take risks. During the Marne-Aisne Offensive he gave me a demonstration on how to explode the detonating caps of German hand grenades (potato mashers). Also he liked to toss pennies on condition that restitution was made after the games. In the dud episode there would have been no restitution if we had lost." I knew my father harbored more than a streak of mischievousness, but I was somewhat taken aback by his obvious daredevil nature as a young man. When I read what William Roth had written, I sighed. So *that* was where my own two boys had gotten the trait that was turning their mother's hair gray.

But very little of those long months in France was given over to fun and games.

Here are parts of a letter he wrote to his brother William on the 28th of July 1918 after the second battle of the Marne.

Dear Brother and all,

As we have been on the go for over a week there has not been much time for writing. But as I don't expect to be called out tonight I am taking the time to write a short note. Perhaps you may be able to read it as I am in my bus along the road writing on a cushion on my lap by candlelight.

We are getting along fine and are again as busy as at first. But are on a front that is moving in the other direction above the old chateau that has made quite a bit of American history of late. We have been going day and night for four days now. But the work is much better at least it seems so when things are favorable. The Americans that were on this front did some excellent work and not only manned their artillery but when they captured a lot of German artillery, just turned the guns around and fired them, also as much ammunition was also captured. That was quite a stunt and has been practiced by others since.

We have seen many prisoners taken and have hauled quite a number of wounded Boche.

I have changed my mind about the quiet night, because they have commenced to go both ways as thick as hops. Perhaps more work tonight.

The souvenir gatherers should be here. They could find anything from a Boche tank to cartridges and the like. I have seen so many helmets, etc., that I would like to get to a place where there are no souvenirs. You have seen the pictures of the forests, how they are torn and ruined; well those are no exaggerations. I saw this after-noon one tree between three and four feet in diameter cut off. And the smaller trees are lying in a tangled heap everywhere. Now and then there will be a shell that did not explode in a tree, while some of the trees are so full of shrapnel and bullets that they are well loaded.

We are well. Our headquarters are in a small town where it was impossible to find enough of good roof left to keep the cooking stove dry. So you see we must sleep in our cars or in dugouts, which are very damp, especially after several rainy days that we have had. Such is life in a place that wherever you and your "Lizzy" keep together you are at home. You never worry about getting back, you are always there. . . .

The wheat, what is left, is very fine indeed, if it could be harvested. Censored by 1st Lt. A.A.S. Your brother,

Raymond

P.S. How does that Overland run now? Ride over and I will race you in my Ford. I know you all enjoy it very much.   R.W.

Roth's memoir includes many details of the 534. Of the dangers they regularly underwent, of the seemingly useless taking, losing, and retaking of decimated villages, of the night drives on rutted roads with no lights burning, and the wasted countryside. In my father's own brief memoir, which he wrote for us children, he says: "It is useless to speak of the horrible slaughter of these fronts."

One of the novels that was hardest for me to write had to deal with the horrible slaughter of war. I almost didn't finish *Rebels of the Heavenly Kingdom* for just that reason. When I hear men bragging about their war experiences I wonder just how much they actually witnessed. The people I have known who, like my father, were in the thick of the horror rarely spoke of it. I finished writing *Rebels* in 1982 and took the manuscript to my father for him to read, but he shook his head and said he'd rather wait for the book. He died a few months before it was published. So I wasn't to know how he would react to the terrible scenes of war that I had imagined but he had lived through.

With fall the section moved up into Belgium, and it was here, on October 31, that my father, who was waiting to take the wounded from a dressing station in Wantgren, was hit in the leg by a shell fragment. Soon afterward the area was gassed, and he pulled off his gas mask in a frantic effort to cover his wound. He knew that

Womeldorf family. My father is the tall one in the back row.

Dad before being wounded.

if gas got into it, it would soon become gangrenous. In telling of the incident, Roth says: "He was an excellent and fearless driver." When I learned as an adult that my father had been wounded on the day that was to become my birthday, I wondered how he might think of that anniversary. He never mentioned the coincidence. Perhaps he didn't want to remember that day in 1918, or maybe he remembered and didn't want to spoil my birthday by speaking of it.

Raymond was taken to a French hospital, which was an old cathedral, where he lay for two weeks. He remembers lying there, unable to speak or move and hearing the doctor who was leaning over him say: "You can forget this one. He's gone already." So he strained every muscle in his body to move something to show the doctor that he was still alive and managed to wiggle a toe.

He and others were shipped to an American hospital, only to find that it was not there. So they simply lay on their stretchers in tents for days until they were finally sent on by freight car to a casino in Boulogne, France, where it was necessary to amputate his right leg just below the knee. His earlier attempt to save his leg had failed and only resulted in damage to his lungs.

On a post card provided by the French army, he wrote:

My dear father and mother and all. I am getting along as well as could be expected. Now don't be all worried and stirred up.

> *Your devoted son,*
>
> *Raymond*

Dad at the hospital.

In Hospitals

Finally, after weeks of recovery in the casino, my father found he could sit up and see across the channel to the White Cliffs of Dover. At Christmastime the nurse brought him a gift of fruit that she said a kind person in Virginia had sent the money for, hoping it could be given to some wounded soldier from Virginia. The donor turned out to be one of his high school teachers. He always cherished this happy coincidence.

"Well," he wrote home, "I'm getting along all right; of course it is a slow process. You should see my rosy cheeks. Every day the sun shines four fellows pick up my bed and carry me out on the veranda. Yesterday I was out in time for a band concert. Everyone is as nice to me as possible. My nurses brought one day steak and mushrooms, another chicken and often fruit from their own mess."

At length he was sent to England, where he was in hospitals in Dartforth and Liverpool before finally being shipped back to the United States and to a hospital in New Jersey.

I think it was while he was at that hospital that he decided to try to visit New York City. He hadn't yet been fitted with an artificial leg, so he was painfully trying to make his way on crutches when a limousine pulled up to the curb beside him and a plump, middle-aged woman with a heavy German accent leaned out and asked him where he was going and if he would like to have a ride. He gratefully accepted and climbed into the backseat beside her. The kind lady proved to be the Austrian opera singer Ernestine Schumann-Heink, who had had sons fighting both for Germany and the Allies during the war.

Several years later when Raymond was in seminary, Madame Schumann-Heink came to Richmond to give a concert. He had no illusions that the famous contralto would remember the ride in New York, but he was eager to see her again. So he went to the concert, and afterward, stood at the back of the formally attired stage door crowd to get a closer glimpse of her. Suddenly, he heard a cry: "My son! My son!" and she made her way through the surrounding fans to give him a warm embrace. It was my mother who told me the story, regretting as she did that he hadn't taken her to the concert.

After his stay in New Jersey, he was transferred to Walter Reed Hospital in Washington, DC. Here he met another noted woman, one who may have saved his life. She was Mrs. Lathrop Brown, whose husband had been special assistant in the Department of the Interior and was currently high up in the Wilson administration. People in the Interior department gave a small portion of their salaries each week to support a convalescent home that was run by Mrs. Brown and a nurse. Mrs. Brown had been a New York debutante, her husband had been Franklin Roosevelt's roommate at Harvard. Needless to say, the eleven fortunate veterans whom she selected for residency received extraordinary treatment. In the summer, she even took her invalids to the Browns' summer place on Long Island for fresh sea air. My mother always believed that left in the crowded wards of Walter Reed, my father would have died. Raymond was under Mrs. Brown's care for several months, living, in his words, "the life of Riley." By the end of October, however, the doctors feared that the gassing may have given him tuberculosis. He needed, they felt, to be isolated and treated for TB.

The friendship with Mrs. Brown did not end when he had to leave the Interior Department's Convalescent Home. She remained in touch with my parents until her death. Every year she would send to us in China a carton of wonderful children's books,

49

a great treasure for a family living "up country" who had no way to purchase books in English even if they'd had the money. She often wrote and even came to China once to visit us. If we were to designate a fairy godmother of our childhood, it would be this gracious lady who saved our father's life and enriched us all. In 1938 when we arrived in New York as refugees, Mrs. Brown was on a trip to Europe, but she had arranged for her chauffeur to meet us at the boat. We must have received our share of startled looks from the crew and other passengers—this seven-member family emerging from their third-class lower deck and climbing into a waiting chauffeur-driven limousine.

After Raymond's time in the convalescent home, there followed a couple of TB hospitals—one in Connecticut and one in the Adirondacks. The current treatment for TB patients was quite literally fresh air—the colder the better. So my Virginia father found himself at a Saranac Lake "cure cottage," where the patients were rolled out on the porch to breathe in the mountain winter air for most of the day. He had lived through gangrene, amputation, and gassing, but now he thought he would surely freeze to death. Among the patients was another veteran from Virginia—a graduate of the University of Virginia. This man realized that illiterate veterans were being taken indoors for an hour or so every day for reading lessons. He proposed that the two of them feign illiteracy and gain a welcome break from the cold.

The ruse worked, at least for a while. Then to Raymond's disgust, his friend whispered something to him that made the instructor look more closely at the two of them. "Have you boys ever been to elementary school?" she asked. They nodded. "Have you had any high school?" They nodded again, this time a bit sheepishly, for the teacher was obviously annoyed. "How much education *have* you had?" she demanded furiously. And when they admitted that they were both university graduates, she immediately called for an attendant to wheel their beds out and force them to face the elements.

By summer, when it was finally determined that, though his lungs were indeed damaged, he was not suffering from TB, he was at last allowed to go home. He had applied and been accepted at Princeton Theological Seminary while he was still hospitalized, but when he told the pastor of the Lexington church this, Dr. Young persuaded him to cancel these plans. In those days the Presbyterian Church was divided as it had been since the Civil War. If, Dr. Young said, he expected to work in the Southern Presbyterian Church, it would be a mistake to go to a northern seminary. Dr. Young took charge, canceled the Princeton registration, and made sure Union Theological Seminary in Richmond, Virginia, would accept his late application. So we children must be thankful to the imperious Dr. Young for making it possible for our parents to meet and our subsequent births.

As I write this I remember a similar event in my own life. While in Japan I was notified of a scholarship for further study that I could use where I wished. I applied to Yale Divinity School, where two of my favorite professors had received their doctorates and was

51

accepted. In the late spring I went to a meeting in Tokyo and an American missionary acquaintance asked me what my plans were for my year in the States. I told him I had been accepted at Yale. "You don't want to go to Yale," he said. "You want to go to Union Seminary in New York City. That's where the exciting things in Christian Education are happening." I protested that it was too late to apply, but he assured me it was not, and with his help I changed my plans. If I hadn't, I would never have become Katherine Paterson.

My parents on their honeymoon.

The Courtship and Wedding

But, of course, I never would have been born at all if my mother had failed to show up as she had been told to at the General Assembly's Training School for Lay Workers in Richmond, Virginia. The semester was already under way when Mary Goetchius arrived that late fall of 1920. The Training School, as it was usually called (causing the public to often confuse it with a juvenile correctional center), had been started just a few years before by professors from Union Theological Seminary. The seminary was strictly for men in those days, but the professors recognized that there was a growing need for a place to train young women who were eager to become overseas missionaries or church workers in the United States.

The Training School was in a large house across the street from the seminary campus, and it was from there, on her first Sunday at the new school, that Mother and her roommate Agnes Rowland set out for the streetcar stop on the way to church services in downtown Richmond. Before the car arrived, two young men from the seminary came to the stop, and Agnes introduced her to Pete Richardson and "Sarge" Womeldorf. No one could quite explain how my father, who was never more than a private, got this nickname at the seminary, but since he was one of the few veterans, and a wounded one at that, perhaps the promotion was a sign of respect from his fellow students.

Soon the streetcar arrived. Mother got on and went to a seat in the middle of the car, only to hear to her horror the tinkling of change in the box by the driver. In her limited experience with Georgia streetcars, there had always been a conductor who came around to collect the fare after the passenger was comfortably seated. One of the young men she had just met had obviously paid for her ride. Her face was red when he came down the aisle. "I guess," he said, grinning, "if I pay your fare I can sit by you."

And so it began. He asked her to take a walk later that afternoon and she agreed. They walked from the seminary to a park almost two miles away, talking and getting to know each other.

He told her much later how important that walk had been. He had not known until that afternoon that he could walk such a distance on his artificial leg.

At what point they fell in love, I can't say. I always believed, listening to the streetcar story, that it was the magical love at first sight. At any rate, by the following year they were engaged. As a child, I considered theirs a great love story, and it was evident to me that they did truly love each other all their lives. In *Jacob Have I Loved,* Louise observes her parents coming off the ferry after a trip they had taken together, and the expression on her parents' faces were ones I often saw on my own parents'. I even gave Mrs. Bradshaw a hat that my mother owned that I thought made both women look particularly beautiful.

Among the letters retrieved from the farm attic is a very peculiar one that my father wrote his mother dated January 23, 1922. He had been home for the Christmas holidays, but apparently had never mustered up the courage to tell his family about two of the most important decisions of his life.

My dear Mother,

It is always good to get news from home and especially a letter from you. There is no place a person looks with more longing and desire to be. You were so good and kind and always have been, so it is no wonder that I think of you all often and long to be there.

Momma I want to tell you a secret that is just for the rest of you and you are the first to know it. Mary Goetchius has agreed to share life with me. She is the most earnest Christian girl and lovable companion and a girl who is loved and respected by everyone who knows her. I know you would like her. She is such an earnest worker; she is a college graduate and was in France in "Y" work.

Momma, I wish I had confided more in you before but I just didn't. But I want to live closer now.

Yes, it has been my intention for a long time to go to the mission field in fact since my sophomore year in college. There is a plenty to do here, but just think of what is to be done on the mission field. I know you will be the same brave mother that sent your boy to France and help me with your advice and prayers to do what the Lord would have me do. That is one reason I told Dr. Young I would come back this summer because I wanted to be home one more summer.

No there will be no wedding until my work down here is completed. I have not said much about her before. But she is loved and honored by all the profs and the folks around, so you see I am not the only admirer, but the leading one I hope. Write me soon what you think, etc.

Your devoted son,

Raymond

P.S. Thank Katherine for the pictures, they came O.K. Tell Joshua I am sending him that suit soon and he can have the coat altered at Lyon's to suit him. R.W.

It seems that my father hit his mother with two bombshells in one letter. The first that he was marrying a girl he might not have even mentioned knowing in previous letters or conversation, and the second that he was planning to be a foreign missionary when he finished the seminary. I don't think his mother ever quite recovered. At any rate, it was obvious to my siblings and me that Grandmother Womeldorf did not really approve of our mother, and that although she and his brothers and sisters wrote to my parents and sent them gifts through the years, they never quite forgave our father for forsaking the family farm. I'll never know what his father thought about all this. I have found no letters from Daddy either to or from my grandfather except that one my father wrote after he was wounded. Grandfather died in 1928, four years before I was born, so I never got to meet him. I once happened to meet a man who said he had known my grandfather and that he'd had a wonderful sense of humor. My father really didn't talk about his parents—just that his father was determined that his children have a good education— so I was pleased to find out where Daddy's own great sense of humor had come from.

Out of the nine children, only my father and his younger brother Herman married and left the farm permanently. Mamie and Maude became nurses and served in the army during World War II, but after the war both returned to live on the farm and work in the local hospital or as private duty nurses in the area.

Katherine graduated from Mary Baldwin College, but her life's work was divided between the farm and teaching classes and catechism in the church. Cora Belle (always known as Cora B.) went to Farmville Teachers' College and taught school while living on the farm. William graduated from Washington and Lee University, but lived out his life as a farmer. Joshua spent two years at W and L, but his struggles with asthma caused him to drop out of college. They never prevented his working long, hard hours on the farm, though. Florence went off to Mary Baldwin but came home after a week, too homesick to continue.

True to my father's word, my parents' wedding did not take place until after seminary graduation. Mother's course was a two-year one, so she spent the year between her graduation and his working in a large church in Atlanta. I'm sorry to say, I've never found the letters that went back and forth between them that year. I would love to know what they were saying to each other while they were separated. But, alas, no such love letters have survived. I do know that he went to visit her during his Christmas vacation and brought presents for her from his family.

The plan for the wedding was a simple one. Mary's older sister had married a Baptist minister who had a church in Gainesville, Georgia. Her sister Helen would be Mother's attendant, and Pete Richardson would be the best man. Incidentally, Pete married Agnes Rowland. The Richardsons and my parents went to China the same year and remained close friends all their lives. The wedding was to be in Mother's sister Anne's home on June 21, 1923.

I have letters from both my aunt Anne and my mother urging my grandmother Womeldorf and any other family members who could be spared on the farm to come to the wedding. I have a vague memory that one of the sisters may have come, but I have no pictures other than a formal one of my mother in her wedding dress and one of Agnes Rowland and Pete Richardson with my smiling parents that might have been taken in Gainesville, so I don't know if any of the Womeldorfs actually made the trip to Georgia.

I have one story from the time of the wedding. It was told to me by my cousin Elizabeth Anne Campbell. She adored her aunt Mary and, at four, was thrilled that her aunt was being married in her house. However, she was a child who wanted attention, and as the wedding day approached no one seemed concerned about her at all. Her baby sister was being cooed over by everyone who came into the house, but no one was cooing over her.

A day or so before the ceremony, the women of the household were bustling about preparing an elegant ladies' luncheon. Again, no one was paying the slightest attention to little Elizabeth Anne, so she decided to go outside and water the lawn. Her mother would be so proud that she was being helpful. Before long the guests began to arrive. One of them, a large woman that she had never much liked, reprimanded her for playing with the hose. The temptation was too great. She aimed the hose directly at the woman's very broad satin-covered bosom. It was most satisfying. She had nothing against any of the other guests, but once she started she saw no way to stop. There was nothing to do but turn the hose against every arriving guest. No one coming out of the house to reason with her was safe either. Even when the bride, her beloved aunt, came out to entreat her to turn off the hose, she could not. By now, it was a matter of self-defense. Regretfully, she soaked the bride's lovely party dress as well.

But concentrating on the bride made her fail to see the dark figure creeping up behind her—a person completely covered by a black, very large man's hat and raincoat, carrying an umbrella as a shield. It was her mother, who turned off the hose and dragged her weeping daughter indoors. It took time, I'm sure, but apparently all was forgiven in time for Elizabeth Anne to serve as flower girl in the wedding itself.

The surest photo I have of these events is one taken of my parents on their honeymoon. They are standing in a field beside a car and Mother's arms are full of mountain laurel. They look very happy.

My parents had been married fifty-five years when my mother died. My father was devastated. "I was supposed to die first," he said, remembering that many people had warned Mother against marrying him because veterans gassed in World War I usually were dead by their early forties. When my father was in his forties he was living a rugged life in China. He died the winter before he turned ninety years old, four years after my mother.

Me at two in Hualian.

Early Days in China

When I was set to go to Japan in 1957, a friend of my mother's, who was appalled that I was heading across the world for four years, asked me: "How could you do this to your mother?" "Well," I answered, "she did it to *her* mother." But when my parents went to China it was different. They were going for seven years without a home leave. It took six to eight weeks just to get a letter home, no one would think of trying to telephone from across the Pacific, and telegraphs were very expensive. Unlike

Japan in 1957, China was a dangerous country. Bandits roamed the countryside, and there was widespread political unrest, which would soon break into actual civil war. I'm not sure how aware the young, idealistic missionaries were of all the physical and psychic dangers they would be facing. My father, as by now you've realized, was fearless, my mother less so, but they were both very much in love with each other and dedicated to telling the good news of God's love to those who had never heard it.

Their honeymoon before heading to China was a long one. They spent the first part in the Blue Ridge Mountains. There followed a lengthy visit to the Lexington farm that might or might not have been delightful. It was never reported upon, so one wonders, but I do know that on August 9, 1923, they left by train for San Francisco.

They had not completed all the shots needed for Asian travel, so the doctor gave them needles and a little vial of serum, and, as Daddy said, "We had a time sticking each other as the train jogged along." There was a memorable stop in Colorado Springs, with a trip up Pikes Peak and a visit to a rodeo, before arriving for a final week in San Francisco gathering the supplies they would need for the next seven years. My father loved peanuts and bought quantities of them to take along, only to find to his chagrin that peanuts were one of China's leading exports. They also went to Chinatown, feeling that since they were headed for China, they should try Chinese food. The only thing on the menu that they recognized was chicken, but when it came the bones were black, so they were afraid to eat it. Again, it was only after living in China that they learned that a certain variety of chicken, one that was considered a great delicacy, had black bones.

They sailed aboard the *Taiyo Maru,* originally a German liner the Japanese had acquired after the war. There was a glorious stop in Hawaii, but six days out of Yokohama, news of the terrible 1923 earthquake reached the ship by cable. Every day the news was worse than the day before. The Japanese crew and the many Japanese passengers had no idea how family members and friends had fared. My mother recalled trying to express concern to one of them, only to have the person cover his mouth and seem to giggle behind it. She had no idea how to react to such a response.

When the ship finally sailed into the harbor the passengers were appalled by what they saw. In my father's words: "Gun emplacements along the way were turned upside down, dead bodies were floating in the water, lots of oil had spilled on the water from broken pipe lines, and the ship could not dock because the dock was no more."

The Japanese passengers were let off the ship, replaced by four hundred and fifty refugees who were taken to an open port and set ashore. Looking up, they had a view of Mount Fuji, its peak lifted above the clouds—an incomparably beautiful sight amidst a scene of terrible devastation.

When at last they reached Shanghai, the city was in turmoil. Workers in the Japanese and English cotton mills were on strike. To blame were two young radicals, a country bumpkin named

Mao Tse-tung and a disillusioned intellectual by the name of Zhou En Lai. These two had had the nerve to ask the owners of the mills to install safety devices so that the children and old people who worked long hours would no longer in their weariness lose fingers and even hands in the machinery. Both the Chinese and foreign owners refused to modify the machinery, and told the troublemakers to mind their own business—hence the protests.

The young couple spent the first year in China in Nanking (now Nanjing) studying the language. I have many letters and pictures from that first year when everything was strange and new. They usually walked to the language school, taking a rickshaw if the weather was bad or they were running late. "One's conscience has many twinges as he rides behind a fellow in a comfortable little buggy and have this fellow pulling you through the mud always going at a trot," my father wrote that first November. "[They] wear no shoes, merely a little straw mat woven to fit the bottom of their feet and fastened with strings. And they go through the winter with nothing more than this."

Their walk to school took them through a graveyard where the mounds were several feel high and cone shaped. Here and there was a stand on which dead babies were placed, the tiny bodies eaten by the dogs that roamed the area. He didn't say so, but I'm guessing most of those little corpses were unwanted daughters.

After a year of study they went to Huai'an, the mission station to which they had been assigned. Lao Tzeo, one of the rickshaw pullers that they had gotten to know in Nanking, was originally from

Huai'an, and he insisted on accompanying them. He thought these two "babes in the woods" needed help and protection in his old hometown. He brought his wife and two small children along, and he became our gatekeeper and she the amah after we children finally joined the family. As my father declared many years later: "They were our trusted and wonderful helpers all the time we were in China."

During those first five years as they continued to study the language, they began their assigned tasks. My father taught in a boys' school and my mother in a girls' school the mission had established. Daddy felt that they should find a property where the boys' school could provide dormitory space as well as classrooms. To his great delight, property was located near the north gate that closely matched his vision for an expanded school. It was the sort of compound that a fairly well-to-do extended Chinese family might own with several small separate dwellings and some open space behind a gated wall.

My parents lived in one of the small houses, the gatekeeper and his family in another. The other buildings and the grounds were part of the school for boys from fifth grade through junior high. Apparently the teachers were reluctant to push the boys too hard—many of them, after all, came from families where no one else was literate. My father was a strict headmaster because he was determined that their boys do as well on the government examinations as boys from government schools. In the first graduating class of seven, among the eight hundred boys taking the exam, six of the boys from the north gate school scored in the top ten percent. The teachers were convinced.

My father loved sports and he was also determined that the boys be physically fit. He introduced basketball. The boys loved it, but basketball is the wrong sport for boys wearing the long gowns that set scholars apart from peasants. By the end of a game, the precious gowns had been stepped on and were dirty if not torn. Needless to say, the parents were outraged. Daddy's solution was to have the boys take off their gowns and play in their skivvies and put the gowns on again before they went back into the street.

All went well until the spring of 1927. The young Communists that my parents had first heard of when they landed in Shanghai were now a force to be reckoned with. Two Russian generals had come in 1923 along with other officers and propagandists from the Soviet Union and helped the Chinese Communists organize and push their way up from Canton to Nanking. They killed several missionaries in Nanking and threatened others, so all the missionaries were told to leave—that if they stayed they not only risked their own lives, but put any Chinese who supported them in danger as well.

My mother was very sick at the time, so the mission decided that my parents should go directly to the mission hospital in Seoul, Korea. The trip itself was a hazardous one. Hundreds of peasants began clambering aboard the dilapidated steamer, causing it to list from side to side. My father and several of the other foreigners

The boys' school photo.

Welcoming Baby Anne in Kuling 1937.

finally persuaded the captain that if any more passengers were allowed aboard, the boat would surely sink, so some of the would-be travelers were left behind. Mother's mysterious abdominal distress had gotten much worse, and she was lying below, doubled over in agony, when another missionary wife sharing her cabin began screaming that they were all going to drown. Mother got so angry that she forgot her pain and just yelled at the woman to have faith and shut up.

Once in Seoul, my mother was admitted to the hospital and taken almost immediately into surgery. When she woke up, the surgeon, who was also a gynecologist, was waiting. "Am I going to die?" she asked. "Not only are you not going to die," he said. "You're going to be able to have children." This was news that both my parents were desperate to believe, as they longed to have children and there seemed to be no answer to why my mother could not become pregnant.

Don't ask me to explain the diagnosis or the cure. Mother put it like this: "Besides taking out my misplaced appendix, he put all my other insides just where they should have been."

And how. Within the next ten years, she had six babies. The first was my brother George Raymond Womeldorf Jr., born the following spring in Shanghai, as the Communists had taken over our compound in Huai'an, and it wasn't safe for women and children to go "up country." My father returned and when he arrived his Chinese friends greeted him warmly and said he should have stayed. "They might have killed you the first day," they said. "But after that they wouldn't have bothered you."

Our compound was occupied, but Daddy and Mr. Yates were allowed to stay in the little office of the boys' school. Every time the two of them went past the house that had been my parents' home, the Communist soldiers cursed them. All the occupiers were young, from about eighteen to twenty-two or -three. The comrade in charge said, looking straight at my father, who was much younger than Mr. Yates, that anyone over twenty-five was too old to have any sense and should be shot. The speaker was a Harvard graduate.

Eventually tensions eased and Daddy was even invited into the office of the head of the communications bureau. The man wanted to show off the elaborate road system he had planned for the district. My father was very impressed and asked when he planned to begin the project. "Well," he answered, "the only thing we lack now is money."

Occupiers left, but new ones came in to take their places in the compound, so it was months before our home was vacated. Before the first Communists arrived, our faithful gateman Lao Tzeo and his wife had hidden all the furniture and sealed off the room with a cat inside to eat the mice and rats that might want to chew on the upholstery. So their belongings were safe, but the house itself was a mess. It had been occupied by sick soldiers who had slept on the floor on rice straw mats. The whole place crawled with a variety of vermin. After a thorough cleaning, Daddy and Lao Tzeo got large earthenware jars, filled them with sulfur, and then closed up the

Me at about eighteen months.

Ray, me, and Liz.

Me at five in Kuling.

house as tightly as possible for three days. If any reader is anxious to know how to get rid of bedbugs, this is apparently a no-fail solution.

When Mother and Baby Ray came home, there was great rejoicing. All their Chinese friends loved the blond blue-eyed baby with a passion and he was dubbed "Didi," which means "little brother." He was only able to shed his baby nickname after he had four little sisters and pronounced in no uncertain terms that he was nobody's little brother. He became a big brother in December of the following year when Charles Bennett was born just before Christmas. Charles was a beautiful, perfect baby who lived only three weeks. Today, what was probably a congenital anomaly would be quickly diagnosed and repaired, but this was 1929, and they were ten miles from the nearest hospital. Because it took mail almost two months to go back and forth from family and friends in America, they were still receiving presents for the baby long after he was dead. "Unless," my mother said in her recollections of those days, "you have gone through the experience of giving up your own baby you'd never understand the grief of it."

The first term of seven years was up in 1930, so that summer the family of three came back to Virginia, where my older sister, Elizabeth, was born, also a December baby, loved and cared for by two grandmothers and a passel of aunts and uncles.

Liz, Helen, Ray, and me (petting baby kid), in Huai'an.

At Home in Huai'an

My mother managed to anchor her peripatetic life by places in China. If it was a big city, she'd call it Shanghai; if it was a vacation spot, she'd call it Kuling; if it was home, she'd call it Huai'an. Even though I left Huai'an when I was not quite five, I always knew what she meant. Huai'an always meant home to me too, though we had fled from home so often over the years that my aunt Anne used to refer to my family as the "China fleas."

The family, now four, returned to China in 1931 to terrible

floods, caused by the Yellow River breaking its banks. The Grand Canal overflowed as well. The dikes around the city of Huai'an were high enough that the city itself was spared, but the surrounding rice fields were covered with up to fifteen feet of water. This meant starvation for most of the population. Any spot of dry ground was covered with shacks housing sick and starving people. There was no place to bury the dead. My father spent the next long year in famine work. His constant companion now was a scholar turned minister, Li Chang Chiang. After the Communists effectively shut down the boys' school in 1929, it never reopened, so there was a house for Mr. Li and his wife and daughter in our compound. He and my father were not only neighbors and colleagues, but the closest of friends.

Daddy and Mr. Li formed teams of five or six men who went from place to place in small boats handing out secretly marked vouchers. They gave these tickets to everyone they saw in need and directed them to go to a certain temple that was on high ground where the wheat, flour, clothing, and seed rice for later planting provided by the China American Famine Relief Committee was warehoused.

One day Charles Lindbergh flew over the area, expecting to land on the water. Fortunately, my father said, he had not cut off his motor before he saw hundreds of little boats racing toward his plane and he was able to fly off safely. People were desperate, and from time to time Daddy and Mr. Li were accosted and held by people demanding food. When it was apparent that they had no food with them, they were let go. At the end of that very long year, as Daddy was writing out the last famine relief ticket, he said to Mr. Li that he hoped it would be the last such ticket he would ever have to write out. "Then you must be planning to leave China," Mr. Li said, "as famines occur every eight or ten years."

Besides the natural disaster, two other tragedies scarred the autumn of 1931. One of the Presbyterian missionaries they knew well was taken hostage and killed by bandits. But even sadder was the suicide of a missionary wife, a special friend of my mother's. In his letter to his family, my father wrote: "Many at home fail to realize the strain under which people live out here."

Once the famine was over, my father was given a new assignment by the mission. Up until that time, the missionaries had been in charge of the Chinese Church, but a new day was dawning. The Mission Board decided that instead of being in control of the work in China, the missionaries should seek to assist the indigenous church. Daddy was asked to work in the area previously served by Mr. Yates, the feeling being that a new, younger man would be better able to effect this change in philosophy than one who had been for many years the man in charge.

My father worked with five Chinese evangelists in the area, but the person he worked most closely with and almost always traveled the countryside with was Mr. Li. Once, in a country village, the hospitable farmer moved his pigs out of the next room and gave it to Daddy and Mr. Li for the night. The next morning Daddy woke up to see Mr. Li shaking his long garment as hard as he could. When Daddy asked him what was going on, he replied that he'd been feeding those fleas all night and now he was leaving them behind to chew on someone else's body. Daddy would shake his head when he told this story. Mr. Li was a gentleman and a fine classical scholar. My father was a farm boy from Virginia who had lived through unbelievable conditions in France and Belgium. For my father, sleeping in a pig room wasn't too much of a stretch, but he just couldn't get over Mr. Li being willing to put up with such a life. It is hard for me to fully realize that my father was living this same life with damaged lungs and an artificial leg, which, we only learned many years later, constantly irritated his stump and made walking painful.

Mr. Li and he made the circuit of the tiny churches in the area. They also went to villages where there were no Christians. In one such village they came upon the village elders seated under a tree sipping tea. As they approached, speaking as politely as they could, the elders ordered them to leave. Just then a man came riding up on a donkey. He was obviously drunk and shouted a hilarious hello to Mr. Foreigner. The surprised elders asked if he knew the big-nosed foreign devil. Oh, yes, he said. He had been healed at the foreign hospital in Tsing-Kiang-Pu. The elders relented and shared tea with the Christians and listened while they told them about the love of God.

The two friends not only talked about the good news of the Gospel, they gave medicine to the sick, food to the hungry, clothes to those in need. My father even pulled out an abscessed tooth

Kuling, August of 1937.

The road up to Kuling.

once at the insistence of the owner. There was also an elderly burn victim that he treated with cold tea leaves who always bragged that it was the preacher who had given her such a beautiful pink skin. He and Mr. Li often traveled by donkey. "It was easy to get off the thing," my long-legged daddy said. "I just put down my feet and he'd walk away."

There was one organized church in Huai'an with seventy-eight members located at the west gate and the tiny chapel in our front yard. In the entire area of about two million people there were about five hundred churches, most of them tiny. My father and Mr. Li had a vision of a strong national church and for this they worked day after day.

My father loved China and was always eager to learn as much as he could about the country, its history and its people. When the Taoist priest invited him to visit the temple, he went. The priest showed him around the room that held the images of various gods, one of which, to my father's amazement, was an ancient but clearly recognizable painting of Marco Polo, who must have visited Huai'an during his thirteenth-century travels about China. The priest asked my father to donate a picture of Jesus for his collection, and, after thinking about it, Daddy did. He didn't think Jesus would mind having a twentieth-century Sunday school portrait displayed alongside the other venerables in the temple.

I was born the year after the famine. I remember those years of my early childhood as idyllic. I began speaking in both Chinese and English as soon as I could speak at all. In the August before my second birthday my father wrote of me: "Katherine is talking Chinese more than the Chinese children are. I believe she is talking more for her age than the other two." I'm imagining my quiet father, who never spoke unless he had something worthwhile to say, wondering what he would do with this child who wouldn't shut up in either language.

Along with the Lis and the gateman's family, there was a widowed woman living in our compound. Her name was Mrs. Liu and I was her special pet. Every day I'd trot over to her little house, timing it for lunch hour, as I was assured of Chinese food at her house and there was no such guarantee at my own. Once my mother said to me as I was on the way out of our house, "If you eat so much Chinese food, you might turn into a little Chinese girl." I stopped to consider this. I loved my momma and daddy and would hate to give them up, but even that thought did not keep me from trotting down to Mrs. Liu's that day or any day.

Perhaps my earliest memory is one from a lunchtime visit with Mrs. Liu. She had told me to wash my hands and I stood over the basin playing in the water for so long that the tips of my fingers went pruney. I was alarmed and ran to show Mrs. Liu how I had damaged my fingers. She explained to me quite gently that it had happened because my hands had been in the water for a long time, but soon they would be good as new. I don't think she had any children of her own, but she remains one of the kind parenting figures from my childhood.

In June of 2000 I was invited to Beijing to launch the Hans

Christian Andersen Award Series of books that Hebei Children's Publishing House had envisioned and handsomely published.

When the editor, a Mrs. Zhang, first approached me about the proposed series, I replied immediately and enthusiastically. Yes, I wanted books of mine to be a part of the project, and, yes, I would plan to come to China to help launch the series when the books were ready. "What you probably do not know," I said in my fax, "is that I was born in Jiangsu Province, and, therefore, it means a great deal to me to know that my books will be read by children in the land of my birth." "When you come to China," Mrs. Zhang replied, "we will take you home."

We launched the series in the Great Hall of the People, built by Mao Tse-tung to celebrate the Communist State. Wouldn't my parents have been amazed that their daughter was speaking in the Great Hall? There followed a conference with writers both Chinese and foreign talking about children's books in their respective countries. At the close of the conference, Leena Maissen, the executive director of the International Board of Books for Young People, Mrs. Zhang, my daughter Lin, who had come along for the adventure, and I took an early morning flight to Nanjing. We were met at the airport by a guide, a driver, and an ancient Volkswagen van. We boarded the van and headed northeast across the city.

Our guide said the great bridge we were crossing had been called one of the ugliest bridges in the world, but to me, whose memory of travel in Jiangsu was of days on crowded riverboats and tiny canal barges, the long Yangtze River bridge in Nanjing looked quite wonderful. Of course, the modern bridge was younger than I am and the superhighway much younger, but when we had to make a detour onto an almost one-lane country road, I was almost back to the China of my childhood.

It was the 29th of May. The harvest of spring wheat was complete. Our Volkswagen bus drove over sheaves, the road being the only place available for winnowing the grain. The fields were already flooded, and while some farm families were in the roadway pitching the wheat into the air, others were planting rice seedlings in the paddies. Now and then a farmer could be spotted behind a rototiller, but just as often it was a water buffalo that powered the plow in the compact fields. After three hours, we came to a bridge that took us across the Grand Canal. The houseboats looked just like the ones I remembered, the same washing hung out to dry above the deck, the fishing gear stowed, the women calling out to neighboring women on nearby boats.

We were in Huai'an before I realized it. The massive city walls that predated the Christian Era had been torn down after the revolution. Now the city sprawled like a great country town, the main streets wide and bustling with cars. There was little to remind me of the ancient walled city of my childhood.

I had asked myself many times before that day, Why am I going back? It had been sixty-three years since I was there and nearly sixty years since my father was there. There would be no one alive who even remembered my family. And there I was taking

Ms. Maissen, Mrs. Zhang, and my daughter Lin to a town far off the tourist track in search of something or someone that was in all probability no longer there. And yet, driving through those fields and crossing over the ancient canal, I felt somehow that I was going home.

At last we arrived in Huai'an. The young pastor of the city's now more than 2,000-member Christian church asked, through our interpreter, "What do you wish to see?" I explained that I knew that my old home and courtyard had been razed, and that I knew it had been many years since any of my family had been in Huai'an, but I was hoping that there might be someone there who remembered my parents. "There is an old pastor here who remembers your father," the pastor replied.

In the courtyard of the old West Gate Church where I had sometimes gone as a child, there was an old man seated in a wicker chair. He looked almost blind, and I wasn't sure at first what he remembered, but at last he began to talk. "There were four families," he said. Since I knew of only three, the Yates, the Montgomerys, and my family, it took me a moment to recall that the first American family to come to the city had left before I was born. "Your parents were the youngest," he continued. "Your father had one leg." I knew then it was indeed my father he was remembering. "I called him Big Brother Wong," he said. "When your father finally had to escape, I was the one who found him a boat. So many years." He shook his head. "So much has happened." And then he began to weep.

Me with Miss Li and Pastor Fei, Huai'an 2000.

Mr. Li's daughter as a teenager.

Just then a white-haired woman came bouncing in on a cane. She spotted me at once and sat down beside me. "We lived behind the same gate!" she exclaimed, thumping her chest. "My father and your father were best friends. They did everything together!" It was impossible. It could not be Mr. Li's daughter. I asked her name, and still unsure, I had her write it down and the interpreter transliterated it into the English alphabet. She was indeed the daughter of my father's best friend, and who, as a teenager, had played with us children when we were small. "I saw you here and I thought I was seeing your mother," she said. I do look like my mother, though I was twenty-five years older than Mother was the last time Miss Li saw her. She asked about my brother Didi and my sisters and shook her head to think that the children she'd played with were now grandparents. "Decades and decades have passed," she said.

We spoke of our fathers. Hers had suffered through war and disappeared during the first Communist purge after the revolution. My father grieved for his friend until his own death. We wept together over our fathers' pain and then laughed with joy that after all these years two of their children could meet. Weeping and laughing with Pastor Fei and Miss Li, I had truly come home again.

Liz, Mother, and Ray. Our Huai'an house.

Enemy at the Gate

Huai'an was home, and in some ways until I'd lived for many years in the same house in Vermont, Huai'an would always be what I thought of as home. And yet, I wasn't quite five years old the last time I saw the courtyard with its moon gate or ran down to Mrs. Liu's house for lunch. There had been rumblings of war with Japan for quite some time, but it broke out in earnest in July of 1937. Our family of seven had gone to the mountain resort then known as Kuling for a few weeks' respite from the brutal heat and humidity of a Hua'an summer. The president of China, Generalissimo Chiang Kai-shek, and Madam Chiang were also vacationing there when we arrived. I was told that we met the first lady on a walk one day, and she patted my sister Elizabeth and me on the head and admired our blond curls. But soon thereafter, the general and his retinue left the mountain. The Japanese had invaded North China. We were at war.

Before the month ended, the Japanese had landed at Shanghai. We could not go home. Three weeks later, my sister Anne was born. The mission decided that the men and single women could return to their mission stations, but the women with children must stay on in Kuling until the situation quieted down. It was a terrible time. Bombers flew over our house nightly while we sat in dark rooms with all the curtains closed, wondering where those bombs would fall. We waited for word every day from our father, never knowing if he was safe or when he might return. I could only imagine how my mother must have suffered with a baby, a toddler, and three children five, seven, and ten who were old enough to be terrified but not, I'm afraid, much help to her.

My father told one remarkable story about that fall he spent in Huai'an. The Japanese army was fast approaching. He had heard stories of the atrocities the invaders had committed elsewhere, so he gathered as many women and children into our small compound as he possibly could, hoping somehow to protect them, though he feared it would be impossible.

I'm sure he could tell from the sounds on the street outside that the army had entered the massive gates of the city. Eventually, there was a knock on the wooden gate of our compound. The gateman asked who it was and was told it was the Japanese commander, who wanted to be let in to speak to the reverend.

The commander came in alone, as I recall the story, and handed my father his card. Then he said in English, "I know you are a Christian. I am a Christian too. I am not sure I can control my men. But if anyone tries to break down this gate tonight, you must send someone over the wall to find me. I will come and try to stop their entering your compound."

That night there was pounding on the gate. My father got a boy, perhaps the son of the gateman, I don't know, handed him the card, and sent him to find the commander. The commander came. He ordered his men to leave the area, and, miraculously, they obeyed.

The infamous "Rape of Nanking" that occurred not long afterward, just 102 miles farther north, tells a story of what might have happened at my childhood home were it not for that commander.

On the beach at Hong Kong before evacuation to the US.

I wrote a book about a family caught in war that had to flee their home and eventually ended up refugees in a foreign land. Our life in China was not as difficult as that of the Lleshi family in *The Day of the Pelican*, but from the time my parents arrived in China in 1923 and all through the years they lived there, China was in constant turmoil. My parents' lives had been frequently disrupted. The evacuation to Korea in 1927 was only one of several dislocations. My parents were painfully aware of the sufferings of ordinary Chinese, but the more fortunate foreigners were not safe. The bandits that roamed the countryside were only too happy to relieve the rich foreign devils of their lives as well as their livelihood.

As a tiny child, secure in the love of my parents and the Chinese friends who lived in the compound that was home in Huai'an, I was blissfully unaware of the things that were happening beyond our gate, but I was to understand it all too well by my fifth birthday.

We had gone to the mountain resort the summer of 1938 and we were caught there when the war with Japan began in earnest that July. Even with the cold weather fast approaching, it was too dangerous for the family to travel, so only my father was allowed to go home. After five frightening months of air raids, news of battles and atrocities, not knowing what was happening to our beloved father, he finally returned. In late January we began our journey out of China. For vacationers, whether Chinese or foreign, there was only one way to get up or down the thousands of stone steps that were the path to the top of the mountain. You rode in a sedan chair carried by two strong coolies. But this trip was only made in summertime. It was January by now and the thousands of steps dug into the edge of the mountain were coated with ice. It was only the sure-footed skill of those carriers that got all the stranded foreigners down that precipitous route without a tragedy. I'm sure that no one breathed easily until all the chairs were safely at the foot of the mountain. There we caught a river steamer to take us to the city of Hangzhou, where we boarded a specially designated train covered with large red crosses.

We traveled from Central China all the way south to British-ruled Hong Kong. The seven of us had spent a week on the journey, and on the evacuation train we were crowded into a single fourth-class sleeping compartment where we both ate and slept. My sister Helen was not quite two and baby Anne was less than five months old. I'm still wondering what my mother did about diapers.

Once we arrived, the British authorities had no idea what to do with this trainload of foreign refugees, so while the fathers were out scouring the crowded city for reasonably priced shelter, the mothers and children just sat on their luggage in the vast lobby of the Peninsula Hotel, which was then and may still be the grandest of all Hong Kong's grand hotels.

Naturally, the elegant British, European, and American tourists who had paid hundreds of pounds for the privilege of staying in the Peninsula were appalled and offended by this filthy lot of women and children who were cluttering up *their* lobby.

My mother, who was not a bitter woman, could not recall that long day without bitterness. "I watched them as they passed by with sneers on their faces and I wanted to cry out to them: 'Do you think I like being here? Do you think I want my children to be dirty?'" She would shake her head. "They couldn't even smile at the baby," she said. "What kind of person can't even smile at a baby?" And she would always end this story by saying, "I can never see a picture of refugees in the paper without remembering how it feels." She later said: "In all the years in China, it was the only time I felt completely sorry for myself."

When I told this story to my good friend Mary Sorum, she said: "Oh, that's why you wrote *The Day of the Pelican.* You remember how it feels to be a refugee." I hadn't really thought about it, but Mary is probably right. The story of the Haxhiu family escaping the war in Kosova and coming as refugees to America that had inspired my novel, must surely have reminded me of that day in the Peninsula Hotel.

I did not remember what happened next. It seems that no place was found in the city for us that day. Someone in the hotel management took pity on the refugees and told the staff to put up cots for them in one of the dining rooms. My father was helping the staff set up the cots, and he said to one of the maids that he had five children, two of them babies. "Nobody wants to sleep with that kind of family," he said. The maid told him to come with her and she fixed up one of the private dining rooms just for us. So after the humiliation of the Peninsula Hotel lobby, we spent several days in comparative luxury in the private dining room.

Our next stop was an abandoned British army barracks and then on to a single room in the missionary hostel, where the cots had to be folded up before anyone could move around the room, except for those of us who thought it great fun to walk from bed to bed without ever touching the floor.

One morning my father took the older three of us out, so

Mother could bathe the babies. I was looking into a shop window when suddenly I realized that Daddy and Ray and Elizabeth had disappeared. In a panic I entered the shop. They weren't inside. I ran into the neighboring shops. They were nowhere to be seen. Terrified, I sat down in the middle of the busy sidewalk with hundreds of feet and legs going past and began to cry. Before long I heard a kind British voice ask if I was lost. I looked up into what I remember as a beautiful woman's face. "Where do you live?" she asked. Somehow the day before Mother had impressed on us the fact that we now lived in "The Phillips' House."

When my new friend arrived at the door of our room with me in tow, my mother's first words were: "But she has a father." To which my rescuer replied: "I'll go back and find him." And she did.

There are things that happen to us when we are children that we never quite recover from. I know that even now, as much as I have traveled, when I am in a foreign city and feel even the slightest bit disoriented, I can feel the panic of that day on the Hong Kong street begin to rise in my chest. My story of being lost ended quickly and happily, but it still haunts me. Young readers look at my nearly white hair and ask: "How do you know how we feel?" And I know because I still carry that child that I was inside myself. She is very much alive.

Ships headed for the States across the Pacific were booked far into the future, but my father discovered that with the favorable rate of exchange, we could go in the other direction around the world for about the same amount of money. We started our trip back to the United States aboard the *Potsdam*, a German liner. At the end of every passageway one ran into an enormous portrait of Der Führer.

I remember the *Potsdam* chiefly because I nearly drowned in the swimming pool and was reprimanded by crew members after my rescue for tracking water on the carpet. Then there was the children's dining room presided over by a diminutive female Hitler of a stewardess. The dessert was some miserable kind of pudding that I loathed. She would stand over my chair and command: "Eat your puddink, Katrina, my luff!" My older brother and sister imitated this command for years, and my mother often teasingly called me Katrina after that.

The fun of the voyage was the ports of call, and there were many: the Philippines, Singapore, Sumatra (where the flags were flying in honor of the birth of the new Dutch princess), Ceylon (where the snake charmer charmed us children), and Suez, where the sight of German warships brought the entire crew on deck to cry "Heil Hitler!" I didn't know who Hitler was at the time, except that he was someone my parents didn't like. Port Said (If it was Africa, where were the lions? I wanted to know), the Mediterranean to Genoa (where we saw where Columbus was born), through the Straits of Gibraltar to South Hampton, England. From there we took the train to London and four days of sightseeing between ships. For me there was one major disappointment and two terrors. First, the royal princesses did not show when we went to see the changing of the guards at Buckingham Palace. I had been sure they would. Didn't they know how much I admired them? The waxworks were scary enough, but when the taxi was about to cross London Bridge I shrieked and refused to go. It was *falling down!* Everybody knew that.

My mother said that tourist class on the *Europa* was more like steerage on an ordinary liner. I hardly remember the *Europa,* but I'll never forget my first glimpse of the land my parents called home. It was the Statue of Liberty. A sight to thrill any refugee, even one five years old.

Mother and Dad in Beijing.

My Father the Drug Smuggler

By the spring of 1939, the Japanese had occupied much of eastern China, and, after our year in Virginia, it was determined that we could return to China. Again, because of sporadic fighting between the two armies, as well as roving bands of guerrillas and the ever-present bandits, women and children were not allowed "up country." The six of us stayed in Shanghai while our father went back home to Huai'an. There the older three of us went to the Shanghai American School, and for most of that time we actually lived in the school dormitory, my brother in the boys' dorm and my mother and the four of us girls in one room of the girls' dorm.

The occupation made the missionaries' work very difficult. My father could not get permission to visit the small country churches that were his and the Reverend Li's chief responsibilities, unless he agreed to report to the Japanese headquarters the number and location of any Chinese soldiers in the area. He refused to do this, so he was pretty well confined within the city walls. Meantime, the mission hospital in Tsing-Kiang-Pu, ten miles away, was running out of medicine and supplies. The doctor in charge, Nelson Bell (later best known as Billy Graham's father-in-law), asked Daddy to go and fetch some that were waiting in Shanghai.

There was no problem with funds. Apparently, the hospital had plenty of money to pay for the needed items; the problem was getting the money safely to Shanghai and then getting the valuable supplies safely back to the hospital. There was another hospital in Taichow in need, and my father was asked to bring supplies back to them as well. He purchased some large cracker cans, put the money in the bottom of the cans, and covered the cash with crackers. He hitched a ride on a Japanese army truck to take him through the next general's territory, where the money would be contraband. He rode the entire way with a machine gun sticking over his shoulder and a bunch of nervous Japanese soldiers on the lookout for remnants of the Chinese army. After a long day's travel, they reached the railway station located within the second general's territory. At the station soldiers opened up a couple of the cans, saw the crackers, and closed them up again while my father stood by sweating and praying the train would hurry up and come.

After arriving in Shanghai, he gathered twenty-five ship tons of supplies (this refers to measurement, not weight, but in any case it's a lot of baggage), enough for the two hospitals, bandages of every description, medicines of all kinds, including the last shipment from Germany of a very rare and expensive drug for black plague. Now the challenge was to get everything to the hospitals without it being confiscated by the Japanese or stolen by bandits or guerrillas. He wanted especially to protect the black plague medicine, so he bought a small steamer trunk, put the small package of medicine in the bottom, and covered it with lots of bandages.

The Grand Canal would have been the preferred way to take baggage up country, but it had been thoroughly blocked by the Chinese army and was unusable. So the plan was to load the supplies onto an American gunboat and take them up the Yangtze River as far as Ko An, where they would be loaded onto a small boat that could navigate one of the back canals.

Just as the gunboat was loaded, a wire came from a missionary at the hospital in Taichow saying that the Japanese had taken Ko An and they wouldn't be able to land there. They should wait until the army cleared out. So Admiral Glassford ordered the crew to unload the supplies from his flagship gunboat, the *Luzon*. Daddy watched the gunboat leave without him. For a while he just stood there, surrounded by his twenty-five ship tons of luggage, until finally he went and found adequate storage space. Many days later another wire came saying the Japanese were dug in and probably wouldn't be leaving any time soon, so Raymond should try to get a pass from the Japanese general to bring the supplies anyway. He knew that although the Japanese had declared the Yangtze closed to foreign shipping, Admiral Glassford was planning to take the *Luzon* on another trip up the river. My father asked for passage once again. The admiral agreed, but despite every attempt, Daddy was unable to obtain a pass. He went to Admiral Glassford to tell him that his attempts had failed, but the admiral suggested that they go ahead and reload the supplies and make another appeal to Major Otori for a pass.

The morning of the day that the loaded gunboat was scheduled to leave, my father made yet another visit to Major Otori's office to plead for a pass. The major who was the liaison between foreigners and the military asked how the supplies were to be carried. When Daddy explained that they were to go by US gunboat, the major flew into a rage, and although my father couldn't understand Japanese, he was quite aware that he and the entire American navy were being roundly cursed. The major was furious that the admiral of the Yangtze fleet would run a blockade and carry goods to Ko An on his flagship. "Give you a pass to land goods at Ko An? Never."

My father went back to the gunboat to give Admiral Glassford the bad news. The admiral said he had a mind to just take the goods and run the blockade with them, but he said, "I see he has you." So once again the gunboat was unloaded.

A week later Daddy heard that a river steamer was going up the river under Japanese supervision. He rushed to make arrangements. One of the missions' single ladies heard he was going and asked to go with him. She would be traveling with two Chinese friends. He said the women could go along with him if they would bring *very little baggage,* as he had this mountain of supplies. When he went to buy steamer tickets for the four of them, he learned that the river was closed, so he got in touch with Miss Jessie and told her they would have to try to go as far as they could by train. They were to meet him at the station an hour and a half before train time with *very little baggage,* as the authorities would inspect every piece. The ladies got to the station on time bringing twenty-four pieces of luggage among them.

Chinese workers under Japanese military supervision carried out the actual inspection. One of the inspectors rooted around in the steamer trunk and came up with the small package containing the precious black plague drug. "What is this?" he asked. My father's heart skipped a beat, but just then a second inspector came over. "Keep quiet and close that trunk," he muttered. "You know that man is not carrying anything that would hurt the Chinese."

The train trip proceeded without incident, but the next day they were to board a small launch that would take them on the next leg of the journey. Once again all that baggage had to be inspected. Daddy had untied the steamer trunk and was going through some hand luggage with the guard when a Chinese helper tied up the trunk and began dragging it across the line to the already inspected side. My father breathed a sigh of relief only to hear Miss Jessie call out: "Wait a minute! The official hasn't inspected *that* trunk yet!"

"I looked daggers at Miss Jessie," my father said, "and told her to keep quiet and let my conscience work this time." Somehow, the trunk was spared, and they were able to board the launch, moving up the Yangtze for several hours until they landed at a small village where my father had to round up enough rickshaws to take the four of them and all the ladies' baggage the five-hour overland trip to the hospital at Taichow. The hospital supplies were left under the care of a Chinese helper who had taken them on the several small boats to the port of Ko An.

In Taichow Daddy was able to finagle two passes—one pass would allow him passage through the territory controlled by a guerilla general and the second would allow him to go to Ko An, now held by the Japanese. After finally arriving at Ko An, he managed to negotiate a "landing fee" so that the Japanese authorities would allow him to unload the supplies brought up by his assistant from the village. Here the supplies were loaded on other small boats. It was a two-day boat trip to Taichow. When Daddy and his assistant saw soldiers on the banks of the canal, they looked carefully to see whether they were Japanese or Chinese so they'd know which pass to pull out.

At Taichow, the supplies for the first hospital were unloaded, one more to go. There were no locks on these small canals, so every time a boat had to go up a level, everything would have to be unloaded and carried to a boat on the next level. Since it was almost impossible to keep track of this procedure with several small boats, Daddy decided to get one large boat that could carry the remaining load to Tsing-Kiang-Pu.

They got it all loaded, but there was hardly any place left to sit or stand except on top of the boat. Things went fairly well until the boat found itself aground in a huge swamp buffeted by a strong north wind when the boat needed to go north. So there they sat sunk in the mire for one day, two days, three days, four. On the fifth day Daddy urged the boatman to try to move. He tried but they only slipped back into the swamp. The area was known for bandits, so the sailors were as eager to move on as my father was. Finally, later on the fifth day, the wind changed and they were able to push the boat out of the swamp.

They moved ahead for a couple of days and then the boat hit bottom again. This time, happily, they were able to maneuver the boat to the bank and were not stuck in the middle of the swamp as before. Daddy and his Chinese helper went ashore to round up wheelbarrows and rickshaws so that they could continue the journey. The large boxes of bandages were loaded onto wheelbarrows, but the next thing he knew they were all unloaded. The barrowmen said they couldn't see over the tops of the boxes. They feared they might run off the path and end up in the canal.

U. S. S. LUZON
At Shanghai, China.
24th April,.40.

Dear Womeldorf.....Your letter from somewhere in China
came along yesterday to cheer my heart with the knowledge that all is well with you and that the things
we were to have taken up river for you, have reached
their destination at long last. I can immagine the reception given both to the supplies and to the lad who
brought them. My only regret is one born entirely of
the desire that I might have had a hand in their delivery.

A letter from Richardson was received a day or so ago.
He wrote from Taichow and told of his son having done
something or other that required medical attention at
Chinkiang. Apparently we just missed him on our last
trip. Have written him that shall leave here again on
Monday the 29th, and that upon arrival off Kowan I
hope to see a junk flying our stars and stripe s .
Since writing to him two days ago my plans have more
or less crystalized. Shall spend a night off Kowan at
all events for a look-see at that situation and with th
hope that I may run across someone down from the interior. I should arrive off Kowan Tuesday evening the
30th spending the night there before running on to
Chinkiang, where I understand from a note recently
had from Mrs Woods that the Doctor has not been well.
Shall have the GUAM with me. She has a new skipper
and this is his preliminary canter on the river. I
may also have the ISABEL in company. Admiral Hart at
the moment is in Shanghai...came up from the Islands
in the Isabel. Yesterday the Augusta arrived so that
the Isabel is more or less hanging in a bight here at
Shanghai. It may be inasmuch as she too has a new
Skipper that the Admiral will wish him to have a fling
at the Yangste. We can provide all of that and more.

It is good of you even to ahn get that I go along with
you on these trips. Of course I should love it...I
really think so. It would be fun no matter what happened.

                                                    back
I expect to pass Kowan again on the return trip/to
Shanghai sometime during the day of the 13th...Monday.

Take care of yourself. Our best to all of you THERE
whom I hope one day to meet.

Things keep stirring in Europe. If there should be
a sudden blast in the Balkans we may have to change our
plans. It would not surprise me if by the time you
get this the fighting should have shifted from the
Skager Rak to the Adriatic. It is my view that the
Germans, the Italians and the Russians will settle all
frontier questions, namely Poland, the Baltic States,
and the Balkans thus incuring and consolidating lines
of communication into Germany, before starting the real
fighting in the West. I think we are on the eve of the
Balkan push. We shall see.

The letter from Admiral Glassford.

G. Raymond Womeldorf Esq.,

Presbyterian Mission, South,

HWAIANFU, KIANGSU.............China.

Envelope of Admiral Glassford's letter.

So they loaded everything else on the wheelbarrows and hired carriers to haul the big boxes. When they got to a village where Daddy could hire three-wheeled ox wagons, they loaded the large crates on the wagons. Then they started the thirty-five-mile trek across to the hospital, three ox wagons, thirty-four wheelbarrows, and a couple of rickshaws for the men. On the second day, they were met at the hospital door by Dr. Bell.

"What took you so long, Sarge?" he asked.

"And what did you say to *that*?" I asked Daddy when he told me the story many years later.

He grinned. "Nothing," he said. "What was there to say?"

Going through some of my father's things looking for pictures, I found a letter to him from Admiral Glassford, dated 24 April, 1940. "Dear Womeldorf" it begins. "Your letter from somewhere in China came along yesterday to cheer my heart with the knowledge that all is well with you and that the things we were to have taken up river for you have reached their destination at long last. I can imagine the reception given both to the supplies and to the lad who brought them. My only regret is one born entirely of the desire that I might have had a hand in their delivery . . ."

The moongate in our courtyard. Mother is holding me.

The Last Year in China

While my father was up country or trying to get up country, the rest of us lived in the dormitories at the Shanghai American School. I recall in September a reporter from the English language newspaper, whose funnies I read religiously, coming to interview students about "the war." Six at the time, I'd already seen more war than I cared to, and, quite naturally, I thought the man meant the war currently raging in China. But, no, he meant the just declared war between Britain and Germany with which I had

had no experience aside from the devoted Nazis on the *Potsdam*. I remember realizing that my confusion as to what war he was talking about annoyed the interviewer and he quickly moved on to another child to talk about the war in Europe—the war that mattered.

That was a hard year for our whole family. Our father was gone most of the time. Our big brother was one of the youngest in the boys' dormitory, and, as we learned much later, being miserably bullied by the older boys. And Mother and us four girls were squeezed into a single room in the girls' dorm.

I began piano lessons that year. It was a large class and we sat at our desks in front of cardboard keyboards on which we "practiced" until called up by the teacher to perform on the one actual piano. I was small for my age and somewhat shy, but, even then, I loved to perform. So on the night of the recital when all our class of more than twenty went up on the school stage and played for a live audience, I was delighted. I played my little piece and sat down again quite satisfied that I had done well. My mother certainly thought I had.

At our next class session, our teacher seemed pleased with the recital. She said that all of us had done well, and she had been proud of us. With a single exception. She sat down on the piano bench and demonstrated, to the glee of my classmates, how "little Katherine Womeldorf" had slid up and down the bench to reach the keys. Our teacher had evidently not learned that a child's feelings might trump even a perfect performance at a piano recital.

Despite the war raging in the countryside and the occupation of much of Shanghai by the Japanese army, life in the French Concession, where Shanghai American School was located, was deceptively calm. There were even moving pictures from America. My mother took us older children to see a movie on the life of Stephen Foster, but when he died, I had to be carried weeping from the theater. Watching Dickens' *A Christmas Carol,* I was so terrified by the ghosts that, once again, I had to be carried out of the theater.

The big film event was the coming of *The Wizard of Oz,* which was to be in glorious Technicolor and starring Judy Garland. All the children staying in the dorms were eager for the great day. My sister Elizabeth, well warned that I did not know proper theater etiquette, made me promise to behave. She knew there would be scary parts and I must promise not to scream or cry if I were allowed to go. No one wanted to carry me out of the theater and miss the show because of me. She would sit next to me and warn me when to hide my eyes and punch me again when she deemed it safe for me to watch. She was as good as her word, and although I did get a glimpse of the flying monkeys that haunted my imagination for some time to come, I did not cry or scream or make anyone miss any of the movie.

I loved Judy Garland. When I walked out of the dark theater into the sun, I *was* Judy Garland. Betty Jean's mother bought a record album of the songs, and the rest of us dorm kids were invited into their room to listen. Afterward we began to reenact the movie in the quadrangle every afternoon after school.

I was sure I would be chosen to be Dorothy. Wasn't I Judy Garland incarnate?

I knew all the songs by heart. But, to my distress, Betty Jean, who had long blond pigtails with a beautiful curl at either end, was the unanimous choice of the crowd. It wasn't fair. Betty Jean was an only child whose mother had the time to brush and pigtail her hair and enough extra money to buy her records. She might *look* more like Dorothy, but she wasn't Judy Garland on the inside like I was. Disappointed, I listened as all the speaking parts got taken by others—the scarecrow, the tin man, the lion—Lizzie was the Wicked Witch of the West, which she played with gusto wearing a cape of my mother's for her costume. There were no parts left for me. "You can be a Munchkin," my sister said.

I bravely sang about the Yellow Brick Road in a high nasal voice, but it was declared that one Munchkin was inadequate, so everyone else must chime in and drown out my solo. The Munchkin role disappeared after the first act, so I mostly sat and watched the others play out the rest of the movie with vigor and delight. I was jealous and miserable.

But not as miserable as I was to become. In the spring when we came out of the dining hall after supper it was still daylight, so the boys my brother's age and a little older began a new game. Workmen had dug a ditch across the quadrangle in preparation for laying a new pipe. The boys invented a game they called "Snake in the Gutter." One of the twelve-year-olds, the bigger, the better, would be the snake. He would stand in the gutter and everyone else would jump across the ditch while the snake ran up and down trying to touch the jumpers. If you were touched by the snake you were DEAD and had to drop out of the game. Betty Jean's mother wouldn't let her play. I sneered at that. The ditch was only about two feet deep and certainly no wider than that. It wasn't really dark yet, and, besides, there was a certain glamour in being included in a game invented by the big boys. But with Betty Jean out of the game, I was the youngest and slowest player—every evening, the first to die.

One day that spring Lizzie and I came home to the dorm room after school to find Mother entertaining a visitor. There was no space for chairs, so the two women were sitting on a bed chatting when we came in. As usual, Mother had the two little ones crawling on and over her as she visited, but when we came in she introduced us to the strange lady as her two older daughters. I hardly had time to be proud to be presented as one of the "older" daughters before I realized that the woman was looking us up and down as though she were shopping for a piece of furniture.

Finally, the visitor smiled at Lizzie. "Isn't she lovely?" she said to Mother. "Such charming freckles." Then she turned her attention to me. "Now, Mary," she said, "you can't tell me this one belongs to you. She doesn't look a bit like the rest of the family. Where did you pick up this little stranger?" My mother sputtered in protest, but I couldn't hear it. I could only hear the visitor's pronouncement. So that was it—the explanation for everything. I had been adopted and my parents were too kind to tell me that I wasn't really theirs. That was why my mother had no time to brush my hair, why Lizzie didn't take up for me in front of the others, why I wasn't beautiful like my mother or brave and clever like my father.

That night when the snake bit me, I just started to walk away. It wasn't worth the struggle. I wasn't thinking of what lay in the gathering darkness beyond the safe school campus—war, crime, beggar children with their dirty hands stretched out—all that was forgotten. I was leaving.

I got to the edge of the quadrangle and was nearing Petain Avenue when I realized that Lizzie had left the game and was running to catch up with me.

"Where do you think you're going?" she demanded, holding her side as she tried to catch her breath.

"I'm running away," I said calmly. I hadn't considered for a minute that when you run away you need someplace to run to. I was just going away.

"What do you mean 'running away'?" She grabbed my arm. She was clearly furious. "It's nearly dark."

"I know," I said. "I don't care." I started to walk away.

"Don't be stupid."

"I'm not stupid. But it's no use staying here. Nobody likes me, and I know I'm adopted but Momma is too nice to say so."

She really grabbed me now and whirled me around to face her. There was fire in her eyes. "You can't run away. I won't let you.

And if you even try, I'll never speak to you again as long as I live."

I considered running away a few times after that, but I'd immediately discard the thought. I couldn't run away. Lizzie wouldn't let me. It was a very comforting thought.

The following summer the family went for a time to the coastal city of Tsing Tao (where they still brew their famous beer). We had the loan of a small cottage right on the ocean. The Japanese had occupied the city some time before and life was relatively calm—except in the early afternoon. Every day starting at one p.m., little landing boats would hit the beach disgorging troops, hundreds of soldiers clad only in loincloths. They ran up the beach shouting and brandishing rifles, bayonets fixed. When the officer told my father about the maneuvers, he said they were practicing for the invasion of San Francisco. We could watch them from the window of the cottage if we cared to, but we were never to be in the yard between one and two in the afternoon.

I don't know what happened, but one afternoon I was playing in the yard with three-year-old Helen when I heard a blood-curdling yell. I looked up and saw an army of nearly naked men rushing up the sand, their bayonets aimed right at us. I grabbed Helen's hand, shut my eyes, and ran as fast as my six-year-old legs would carry me to the kitchen door, dragging my little sister behind me. For the rest of the summer, I never again let one p.m. sneak up on me.

In the fall my parents were reassigned to Zhenjiang (known in those days as Ching Kiang), which is the port city where the

Yangtze River meets the Grand Canal. After the one dorm room at SAS and even our tiny home in Huai'an, our new accommodations went to the other extreme. They comprised an entire wing of an abandoned hospital. It was a bit spooky, to say the least. In

Huai'an. Three not so happy little Womeldorfs.

Huai'an I'd been the child lingering at the door while Mother taught Ray and Liz. Now I was studying the Calvert Course third grade. The Bridgmans lived in the house across the narrow valley, and since they had children Lizzie's and my age, Mother and Mrs. Bridgman split the day. We had the morning with Mother and then the four of us would walk down the hill and up to the Bridgmans', where "Aunt" Eleanor would teach us in the afternoon.

The walk each day between the hospital and the Bridgmans' house took us through the village graveyard; the farmers' huts were at the upper end. I'm not sure if all of us light-haired children were more stared at than staring, but I was fascinated by the burials. I couldn't help but stare at the women rocking back and forth, keening so loudly that it echoed across the valley.

Our most frequent visitors at the hospital were the Japanese officers who would come often to interview my parents. My mother always served them tea, just as she would any guest. But our most welcome visitors were the Americans from the US gunboats that patrolled the Yangtze. Admiral Glassford was a particular friend of my father's. He let us children tour his gunboat and gave Lizzie and me ribbons from sailor hats that had *Luzon* embroidered on them. I kept mine for years. I have a memory that when we were ordered to leave China at the end of 1940, we went down by night to the port and took the *Luzon* to Shanghai. I recall that walking on the pier, I could see the reflection of the moon through the cracks between the boards, which somehow frightened me. But there is no record that this midnight gunboat ride ever happened, so I may have dreamed it. At any rate, I always thought of Admiral Glassford as our guardian angel.

Me at six in Richmond, Virginia.

At Home in an Alien Land

People from seasoned journalists to curious fifth graders nearly always ask me about my Chinese childhood. It seems so exotic to have been born there and to have spent my early years there. But that part of my childhood doesn't seem exotic to me. It was the only life I knew and, until the war began, I had a very happy childhood. It was America that was the alien land, exotic from the distance of half a world, but close up, a strange, unfriendly country. To try to clarify the chronology of my complicated young life,

I need to say that we fled China twice for the United States—the first time was 1938, when I was five; the second time at the end of 1940, when I was eight.

By the time I was five I had been through war and evacuation, but nothing had prepared me for the American public school system. In the last few months of my kindergarten year, we "China fleas" landed on my long-suffering aunt Anne Campbell and her family in Lynchburg, Virginia. There, Ray, Liz, and I went to Garland-Rhodes Elementary School. I recall the kindergarten teacher as a dragon lady who constantly belittled me, but, to my amazement, she declared that even though I was only five I was ready for first grade because I could already cut with scissors, a skill I'd mastered with some difficulty at the Chinese kindergarten I'd attended in Kuling. She didn't mention that I could read fluently. She probably had no idea that I could, so that fall when we moved to Richmond, Virginia, to an apartment complex for missionaries on furlough, I entered first grade as a small, extremely shy five-year-old whose curriculum sentenced her to the early Dick and Jane readers. Dick and Jane seemed like a foreign language to me. The books I read at home were stories that made sense. These books at school made no sense whatsoever, and since my classmates were stumbling through them, I imitated their stumbling and was regarded as a slow reader.

I only remember one classmate from the first grade at Ginter Park School. Her name was Martha and she had a beauty mark on her cheek beside her lip. She was the queen of the class, and although I didn't know much about Valentine's Day, I knew that everyone was expected to give Martha a valentine. When the valentines were passed out, the pile on Martha's desk proved that everyone, including me, had complied. I waited a bit anxiously, but the valentine delivery boy passed by my desk every time without putting anything on it. I don't think I was particularly surprised. I understood somehow that I was invisible in that class. But on the way home I realized that my brother and sister were carrying the valentines they received, which they happily showed off to Mother as soon as we arrived. I was embarrassed when she asked to see mine. I hated to confess that I didn't have any to show. It seemed like a character flaw. But Mother was outraged. "How could any teacher let a little girl come home from first grade without a single valentine?" It was a question she pondered more than once over the years. After I was an established writer she asked me why I didn't write a story about the day I didn't get any valentines.

"Why, Mother," I said. "All my books are about the day I didn't get any valentines."

I was happy to be going home to China not long after that. Of course, with all the fighting, we couldn't go home to Huai'an and stayed in Shanghai. The first grade at Shanghai American School that spring was busily preparing for the circus. Since I was small but no longer invisible I got to be the bareback rider atop the first grade's largest boy. I was a star!

The second time we were evacuated to the States, in December of 1940, I was glad to be in a country where occupying soldiers didn't run across our front yard or question my parents—where no bombs were falling and our father would come home safely every night. The few months we spent in Lynchburg, where we once again landed on our Campbell relatives until we found a tiny apartment nearby, were happy ones for me.

This time at Garland-Rhodes School I had a wonderful third-grade teacher and a second cousin in my class who was a real friend. After playing a bareback rider and a firefly in Shanghai American School productions, I was ready for the big time, so I was thrilled when the teacher cast me as the wicked fairy in the third-grade production of *Sleeping Beauty.* I overheard her after my exuberant performance telling my mother, "Katherine really raised the roof!" I half knew it was a compliment, but it was also a bit of a London Bridge moment when I had to worry about the structural integrity of the auditorium.

The next fall we moved to Winston-Salem, North Carolina, and I was enrolled in the fourth grade at the Calvin H. Wiley Elementary School, leaving my kind teacher and cousin behind. The fourth grade was a time of fear and humiliation for me. Nothing I had learned in my previous schools seemed to matter in this one. The Locker Method of handwriting that I had finally caught on to in Lynchburg was invalid in Winston-Salem, where the Palmer Method was the only proper system. Spelling words using the wrong kind of cursive letter were defaced with large red *X*'s even when spelled correctly. The lunches my mother made were nothing like those of the other girls', whose mothers somehow cut off all the crusts from the sandwiches and included cupcakes and other delicacies. Mine might be a thin slice of bologna on crusted bread. One day to my delight there was an egg in my lunch box. I cracked it on the table with gusto, and saw, to my horror, that Mother had mistakenly put in a raw egg rather than the one she had boiled for my lunch. On those occasions when I was given lunch money, it was always fifteen cents, which I am sure was all my parents could spare. I remember vividly a lecture by the teacher on lunchroom duty about my failure to buy a balanced meal. Fifteen cents didn't buy balanced meals in the cafeteria, but it would buy my favorite lunch, which consisted of a bottle of chocolate milk, a small dish of black-eyed peas, and a box of chocolate-covered raisins. I suppose I could have skipped the Raisinets and bought another vegetable, but what nine-year-old would want to do that? And worst of all there was Pansy, the seventh-grade bully, who, along with her two large friends, terrorized me on the playground. Since there were no girl friends to hang out with during recess, I would stand trembling as close to the school building as I could, watching Pansy and her friends coming toward me from the bottom of the huge playground.

"I'm going to report you," she said to me one day. "You're walking on the grass."

I looked down at the hard, bare ground under my feet. "There's no grass here," I protested.

"Of course not," she said, "because people like you keep walking on it."

Being "reported" was like being indicted for a felony. I lived in dread for days. I couldn't tell my parents, they had gone to my aunt Katherine's funeral in Lexington. And even after they returned, I couldn't tell them. The disgrace would have been too much for them to bear.

Every recess Pansy would tell me that any moment now I would be called to the principal's office. One day I was so frightened that I broke into tears in music class. Mrs. Obershein, the beautiful music teacher, quietly took me out into the hall and gently asked me what was the matter. I blurted out my crime and Pansy's threat. She didn't laugh. She didn't even smile. She simply assured me that I would not be expelled for walking on the imaginary grass, indeed she was quite sure I wouldn't even be reprimanded. I should just go to the girls' room and wash my face and come to class when I felt better. If only my classroom teacher had been this warm and understanding.

I recognize now that some of my best writing has its seeds in that awful year, but I can't remember once saying to my nine-year old self: "Buck up, old girl. Someday you're going to make a mint out of all this misery."

There were, however, a few people that I remember with great fondness from that horrible year. One was, of course, Mrs. Obershein, who not only taught me how to do-re-mi, but also showed me that there were adults who could deeply empathize with a child's irrational fears. Another was the librarian of the Calvin H. Wiley School, who made the library a sanctuary and a source of comfort and delight in an otherwise frightening place. And there was Eugene Hammett, the other weird kid in the fourth grade. I have told the story of Eugene so many times that I am sure there are people who could lip-sync it, but I can't resist telling it again here.

Though Eugene and I became friends sometime in the course of that year, there was an important difference between us. I was weird through no choice of my own. I spoke English, as my friends in Shanghai had, with something of a British accent. I could, as I noted, hardly afford lunch, much less clothes, so my classmates would, from time to time, recognize on my back one of their own donations to charity. On December 7, the Japanese attacked Pearl Harbor, and because it was known that I had come from that part of the world, there were dark hints that I might be one of *them*.

Eugene, on the other hand, was weird by choice. Or mostly by choice. I guess he didn't choose his looks. He was a perfectly round little boy who wore full-moon, steel-rimmed glasses, long before John Lennon made them acceptable, and sported a half-inch blond brush cut. My only ambition in the fourth grade was to become somehow less weird. Eugene's declared ambition was to become a ballet dancer. In North Carolina, in 1941, little boys, even well-built or skinny little boys, did not want to be ballet dancers when they grew up.

Now, sometimes outcasts despise even each other, but Eugene and I did not. We were friends for the rest of the fourth grade and all of the fifth, sixth, and seventh grades. During my public school career, Calvin H. Wiley was the only school I went to for much more than a year, and by the time Eugene and I were in the seventh grade, I had fulfilled my modest ambition. I was no longer regarded as particularly weird. I made friends, I wrote plays for my classmates to act out on the playground, my teachers began to realize I was actually intelligent, and, amazing as it seems, in my last year at Wiley School I was elected president of the student body. Eugene, on the other hand, continued to march, or should I say, dance, to a different drummer.

We moved the summer after my seventh grade. I grew up at last and had a full, rich life in which people loved me and didn't call me names, at least not to my face. But from time to time over the years I would think of Eugene and worry about him. Whatever could have happened to my chubby little friend whose consuming passion was to become a ballet dancer?

Me in junior high school in Richmond.

After many decades and scene changes, the Paterson family was living in Norfolk, Virginia, and our son David had become, at seventeen, a serious actor. But in order to get the parts he wanted, he realized that he needed to take dancing lessons. There was, however, a problem. Even in 1983, boys in Norfolk, Virginia, did not generally aspire to become ballet dancers. He asked me to find out about lessons he could take without the rest of the soccer team knowing about it.

My friend Kathryn Morton's daughter took ballet, so I said to Kathryn, "David needs to take ballet lessons, but he's not eager for all his buddies to know about it. Do you have any recommendations?"

"Well," said Kathryn, "if he's *really* serious, Gene Hammett at Tidewater Ballet is the best teacher anywhere around. Of course, you may find him a bit strange, but—"

"W-w-w-wait a minute," I said. "Gene who?"

"Hammett," she replied. "He sends dancers to the Joffrey and New York City Ballet and Alvin Ailey every year. He's especially good with young black dancers. Terribly hard on any kid that he thinks has talent, but he'd give his life for them."

"Gene who?" I asked again.

"Hammett," she said. "You may have seen him around town. He's enormous and wears great flowing caftans. He does *look* a bit weird, but he's a wonderful teacher."

"You don't happen to know where he came from?"

"Well, he came here from New York."

"New York? He wasn't a dancer?"

"Oh, yes. He was quite good in his time. You wouldn't know it by looking at him now, but he was a fine dancer twenty, thirty years ago."

"You wouldn't happen to know where he grew up?"

"Oh, I don't know," she said. "North Carolina somewhere, I think."

"Next time you see him, would you ask him if he remembers anyone named Katherine Womeldorf from Calvin H. Wiley School?"

Some days later the phone rang. "Katherine?" said an unknown male voice. "This is Gene Hammett."

"Eugene! Do you remember me?"

"I even remember a joke you told me in the fourth grade. I asked you why if you were born in China you weren't Chinese. And you said: 'If a cat's born in a garage, does it make it an automobile?'"

"And what about you? You danced in New York, and now you're a famous teacher of ballet. It's hard to imagine. You were a little round boy when I knew you."

He laughed. "Well," he said, "now I'm a big round man."

I saw Eugene a number of times after that, and he was a big round man. But I also saw pictures of him, leaping like Baryshnikov from the boards of a New York stage. And even if I missed knowing him when he was slim and gorgeous and at the height of his career, I wouldn't give anything for knowing that it happened as he had determined it would, back there when we were both weird little nine-year-olds at Calvin H. Wiley School.

I've tried a couple of times to put Eugene into a novel, but I've found that you can't put real people into books. Characters in books have to be believable, and real people, especially people like Eugene, are simply not believable.

I did try to put Pansy, the seventh-grade bully, into *Bridge to Terabithia*. It was going to be the perfect revenge for all those terrifying recess hours she caused me, but, there, again, I don't know why Pansy was a bully. I know that people aren't born bullies, and that no one is a bully or a snob who is comfortable with himself or herself. But I had to know why Janice Avery was a bully, and when I knew, I felt sorry for her. Before I finished the book, I rather liked her. It ruined my plan for revenge. I heard somewhere that unless you can find yourself in your villain, he or she will remain a cardboard character. Good advice for fledging writers, I think.

We had to move after I had finished the seventh grade at Wiley School. The house the church had rented for us was sold and two moves later we ended up living totally across town, so I began eighth grade again with no friends. It might have been a terrible year for me, except for Pat Sewell and Jeannie Snyder. They were best friends, but somehow decided to adopt me as their other best friend. Not long afterward, Audrey Lindner arrived at Gray High School, and the three of us adopted Audrey as the fourth best friend in our little crowd. Unlike most of the girls in the eighth grade, the four of us were still girls rather than adolescents. None of us had a boyfriend, and we hadn't begun to long for male attention.

After eighth grade, we thought we were returning to China and left Winston-Salem. I lost touch with Pat, Jean, and Audrey, but I've never forgotten them. I still have the pictures taken on my little Brownie box camera of the week we spent at Pat's family vacation house on Manteo Island. Pat's mother was a wonderful hostess for four thirteen-year-olds. She took us to see where the Wright Brothers had made their historic flight and to a production of *The Lost Colony*, introducing us to the romantic mystery of the disappearance of those early settlers. All four of us longed to grow up to be actors in that great outdoor drama. One morning there was a contest to see who could eat the most pancakes. I won.

In the years since 1946, I have been able to make a number of remarkable friendships with persons who have changed and enriched my life immeasurably. I think this inestimable gift dates back to Gray High School and the unselfish way Pat and Jean welcomed me into their special friendship, and then helped me welcome Audrey into our circle. My observation has been that thirteen-year-old girls don't often reach out like this. I'd love to be able to thank them for teaching me how to be a friend.

Three schools later when I was a junior in high school and we moved to Charles Town, West Virginia, this magic of friendship happened again. Barbara Hughes was the most popular girl in the small school, and rightly so. Even as a teenager she was one of the most caring people I have ever known. If I had been a weird little kid in the fourth grade at Wiley School, I was certainly a weird big one as a high school junior in West Virginia. I had come from a number of unknown places, most recently from a large high school in a big city. Most of the students had been in school together since first grade.

My father was traveling for the mission board and was rarely home, and my mother was in poor health. I had left friends and a fine high school in Richmond. My unhappiness with the move and my natural shyness made me appear, as I was later told, snobbish. But Barbara took me under her wing, and because Barbara liked me, everyone else had to at least tolerate me.

She married while in college and her name became Barbara Thompson. Thompson Park, the place where Gilly Hopkins finds herself accepted just the way she is, is named in Barbara's honor.

Grandmother Goetchius as a young woman.

Grandmother Goetchius

Although I was at last able to make friends in America, there was one person very close to me that I had great difficulty getting along with—my grandmother. Of one thing I am very sure: When I speak about my grandmother, I am never fair. She was, in the eyes of most people who knew her, a remarkable woman. I didn't want a remarkable woman, I wanted the warm lap and unconditional love other people got from their beloved grandmothers. My first cousin Mary told me once that she thought she and I had had two different grandmothers. She was quite right. She and her older sister Elizabeth Anne were the first two grandchildren. They never knew a time when Grandmother was not a loving presence in their lives, and I am quite sure that Grandmother provided for them the warm lap and unconditional love that every child longs for.

It was a different story when their brother Charles came along. Grandmother had never had a son, much less a grandson, and Charles was all boy. She had no idea how to deal with such a creature. Young Charles was always hoping for the kind of approval she lavished on his older sisters, but nothing seemed to please her. One day in his adventures he came upon a lovely green snake. The perfect present for Grandmother, he thought. He still remembers her scream.

Mary and Elizabeth Anne loved their brother and tried to help their grandmother understand that, despite his total lack of academic zeal, he was really a great guy. Charles was a high school football star, so the sisters decided to take Grandmother to a game. If she could only see him in his element, she would appreciate him more. Unfortunately, the elements of the chosen day did not cooperate. It was a wet day and the field was a muddy morass.

Grandmother's horror increased by the minute, watching these man-sized boys grabbing each other, throwing each other down, and rolling about in the mud for no apparent reason. The older sisters were caught up in the game and when Charles made a spectacular saving tackle, they cried out: "Did you see that, Grand-mother? That was Charles!"

But all Grandmother could see was the depths of depravity to which mankind had fallen. "Oh, daughters," she mourned, "to think they were made in the image of their Creator."

Perhaps the chief source of my difficulties with Grandmother is that I met her for the first time when I was five years old. I read-ily admit to stubbornness, pride, jealousy, and a terrible temper. Indeed, I plead guilty to any of the seven deadly sins available to a five-year-old. Grandmother saw me, not as a grandchild to dote on, but as a wild thing, desperately in need of straightening out before it was too late. My mother, apparently, was not adequate for the task, so it was up to her. We weren't in the country long enough for her to complete her mission, so when we came back the second time when I was eight, she took up her assignment in earnest.

One of her favorite admonishments to me was "Be sweet, my child, and let who will be clever." Well, I didn't want to be sweet, I wanted to prove myself clever, especially since those American teachers of mine thought me a bit slow.

I may have been shy in most public settings, but at home, as the middle child of five, I did whatever it took to get my share of attention, and sweetness didn't do the trick. Worse yet, if there was any opportunity at home, at school, even at church to show off, I would—much to Grandmother's distress. Ladies, even small ones, did not show off.

Grandmother had no home of her own in those days. So her daughters' homes became her homes. From the time I was nine until I graduated from high school, Grandmother lived with us for four months out of every year. We children dreaded these visitations. Our mother would become more and more tense as our family's turn drew near, because I wasn't the only person or thing Grandmother would begin working on as soon as she walked in the door. She'd start by rearranging all the pictures and whatever furniture was light enough to move, and then start trying to rearrange Mother and the five of us children.

The only person spared criticism and improving instruction was Daddy, whom she adored. He could do no wrong. She became almost starry-eyed when she talked to him, and she basked in his attention. Daddy couldn't resist teasing her. We'd watch with fascination the exchange between them at mealtimes. Surely, Daddy had gone too far with his joking. Grandmother couldn't possibly appreciate his wry sense of humor. He'd surely hurt her feelings, she'd stop worshipping him, and then we'd really be in trouble. We were wrong, of course. At first she'd look puzzled, and then she'd break into a coy smile. "Oh, Raymond," she'd say, "you're *teasing* me."

By the time I reached the last years of high school, Ray was in the navy and Liz was in college. So I was suddenly the oldest child. During my junior year, we moved to Charles Town, West Virginia, and were living in an upstairs apartment. Daddy was traveling for the mission board and wasn't there to help with anything, much less Grandmother's visits. Until Barbara and I became close friends, I was totally miserable in Charles Town. Often I would come home from school, and, without even taking off my winter coat, throw myself down on the living room floor to read my current book.

The particular day I remember best, I was totally engrossed in *A Tale of Two Cities*. I guess I was vaguely aware that my mother was sweeping the floor around my prone body, but I was too lost in the book to care until I heard my grandmother's voice, weary with the burden of having failed to make me over, "Sweep, sweep, sweep," she said. "You are going to kill your mother."

I'm sure I should have felt guilty. I was simply annoyed. Grandmother should have been proud to have a grandchild so absorbed in a classic that she ignored the world around her. My mother loved to see me read, and I was quite sure my reading was *not* going to kill my mother, whatever Grandmother might say. And if you're guessing that I had the grace to get off the floor and give my mother a hand, you'd be wrong. It was at about this time that Grandmother seemed to accept the fact that improving me was a lost cause, announcing sadly to Mother: "I'm afraid Katherine is a lover of luxury."

But I started this by saying that I have never been fair to my grandmother. She *was* a remarkable woman, and I have stories to prove it.

After the difficult birth of her third daughter, Grandmother "enjoyed ill health." Mother recalled countless afternoons when she came home from school that she was hushed by the African American housekeeper with the warning that her mother was resting. But Grandmother didn't spend all of her time abed. She was, apparently, noted in Rome, Georgia, for her good deeds. There was a tiny apartment connected to the house, and Mother recalled that it was nearly always filled with some pitiful person or another who would otherwise have been homeless. Every month she sent money to Dr. Harry Myers, a friend who was a missionary in Japan. Dr. Myers wrote that her gift was being used to support a penniless student named Toyohiko Kagawa.

Kagawa went on to become known worldwide for his work with the poorest of the poor in the slums of Kobe and Tokyo. He was imprisoned on a number of occasions because of his activism on behalf of labor and because he opposed the Japanese military, going so far as to apologize publically in 1940 for Japan's crimes against China. He was a prolific writer, often using his time in prison to write, and was nominated both for the Nobel Prize in literature and the Nobel Peace Prize. After his death, the Japanese government, which had so often opposed him, awarded him the Order of the Sacred Treasure, its second-highest honor. Dr. Kagawa died soon after I arrived in Japan, so I never met him. But I was in Tokushima Province when his widow brought part of his ashes to bury them in his hometown. I was able to tell her about my grandmother's pride in having played a part in her great husband's life.

After her daughters had all grown up and left home, Grandmother wanted to be useful. She ceased her role as a Victorian semi-invalid and moved to Baltimore, where, I was told as a child, she became a "missionary to the Jews." The word "missionary" was not a derogatory term in my family, but "missionary" is a misleading description of what she actually did. It seems that the Presbyterian Church was very concerned for the immigrants in Baltimore, many of whom were Jews, who in the 1920s and '30s had fled Europe and settled in the city. Grandmother's job was to teach English to a group of Jewish women immigrants. I think it was a volunteer position, rather than a paid one. One remarkable thing about my grandmother was her ability to manage on very little money

She grew quite close to the women she worked with. One of the rare lovely memories I have of my grandmother is listening to her describe her Jewish friends preparing for Passover. She was awed by the way they approached this sacred rite—the beauty, the purity of it. She'd never seen anything like it in her own church. She was sure, she said, that the Holy Spirit was present with these wonderful women.

Often she would take my mother's letters from China and share them with her friends. She remembered that awful time when she had been in too big a hurry to read the letter first, had simply opened it, only to find herself reading aloud my mother's account of little Charles's death. If my grandmother was broken-hearted, so were her friends. "How can God let a little baby die so far away from his beloved grandmother?" one of them cried as they wept with her for her husband's namesake that she would never know.

I think Grandmother left Baltimore about the time we moved to Winston-Salem. Perhaps if she'd stayed and been nourished by her friends and the work she did there, she and I would have had a different history. I'll never know.

Grandmother lived to be ninety-six, but in 1955, when she was eighty-seven years old, she was living with my aunt Anne in Alexandria, Virginia, and running about visiting sick and elderly friends in Washington, DC. Anne often said, "Mother, you have to watch for cars in the city. You aren't careful." To which Grandmother would invariably reply: "Nobody is going to hit an old lady." But, one day she stepped off the curb and somebody did. Her hip was shattered. A skillful surgeon put it back together and she was able to walk again, but something happened to the grandmother I knew in the process.

After the operation, the iron lady that had frightened and judged me for most of my life simply disappeared, leaving the sweet granny I'd always longed for. I went to see her before I took off for Japan. She seemed particularly fuzzy that day, so I said, "Grandmother, do you know me?" She peered at me closely. "No," she said, settling back in her chair, "but I know you're somebody nice."

My older sister Liz thought she saw Grandmother in Louise's grandmother in *Jacob Have I Loved,* but I really didn't. Louise's grandmother is closer to the mother-in-law of one of my friends, who in her dementia was cuttingly cruel. Until her accident that softened her personality, my grandmother was not demented. She was stern and used Scripture to bolster her arguments, but she was not intentionally cruel. To hint that she was would have been totally unfair to that remarkable woman.

An example of the brass buttons from the Confederate uniform.

Two Brass Buttons

By now you will have realized that my relatives were all Southerners. My father's grandfathers Womeldorf and Clements were Virginia farmers and never owned slaves. Grandfather James Clements (sometimes spelled *Clemens*) was the younger brother of John Clements, who left Amelia County for Missouri and became the father of Samuel Langhorne Clemens in 1835. Which makes me in Southern relative counting, the first cousin twice removed of Mark Twain, if the family history is to be believed. Grandpa Clements lived past his hundredth birthday. He was not a Union sympathizer, but he did not believe in either slavery or war, so he paid someone to join the Confederate Army in his place.

My mother's grandparents, coming from Georgia and Alabama, were Confederates through and through. Great-Grandfather Daniel was a slave owner, although my grandmother told me that he granted them all freedom in his will. Which sounds nice until you consider that he made sure he had their service all his life. Since I have yet to meet an African American named "Goetchius," I don't believe my other great-grandfather was a slave owner, but one of my favorite "kitchen sink stories" comes down from Goetchius family lore.

Slave owners or not, the fact remains that all my ancestors were from the South and some even fought and died for the losing side. Perhaps that's why I was long resigned to my failure to publish. Southerners are much more comfortable with losing than winning. It seems more romantic, somehow. And now for one of my favorite family stories.

My grandfather Goetchius's two eldest brothers, John and Edward, were both killed while serving in the Confederate Army. This story is about John, who was a private in the 2nd Georgia Battalion Infantry.

I had always been told that John had taken part in Pickett's Charge, the bloody assault on Cemetery Ridge on July 3, 1863. Actually he was mortally wounded very close to Cemetery Hill on July 2 the day before that tragic charge. He was carried by unknown hands to a Union field hospital, where a chaplain, who was ministering to the injured, realized that the young man was dying and asked him if there was any message he would like to send to his loved ones. John asked him to cut two of the brass buttons off his uniform and take the flags from his lapels and send them to his parents and his sweetheart.

He lived long enough to give the chaplain his name—John Goetchius—but died before he could tell the kind man where his home was.

For many years the chaplain carried the two brass buttons and Confederate flags around in his pocket to remind him of his unkept promise. Then one day he happened to be boarding a ferry boat somewhere in the South and heard the African American ferry boat attendant greet an elderly gentleman as "Marse Goetchius." The name was so unusual that the chaplain immediately approached the stranger. He introduced himself and asked if by any chance Mr. Goetchius had lost a relative in the Battle of Gettysburg. Yes, the old man said, one of my sons died there. The chaplain produced the buttons and the flags, and later accompanied my great-grandfather to Gettysburg. They found the trench where the dead Confederates were buried, I was told, because the corn was so much greener there. How long it took, I have no idea, but they found my great-uncle's body, identifying the remains by the dental work, and took them home to be buried in the family plot.

My mother was born more than thirty years after her uncle's death, but she remembered John's fiancée, who carried the brass buttons with her always and reminded the Goetchius girls that she should have been their aunt.

Article in Episcopal magazine about Maud Henderson.
Courtesy of the Archives of the Episcopal Church, USA.

Maud Truxton Henderson

During the time we lived in Charles Town, West Virginia, we had a visit from an old friend from China days. Her name was Maud Henderson. Maud had spent most of her life saving those Chinese baby girls that their society had too often regarded as disposable. Mother told me the story of how she had stood at the gate of her compound and told the Japanese soldiers there that if they tried to come in and get her girls, they would have to do it across her dead body. This story alone made her one of my child-

137

hood heroes. Maud felt particularly close to my parents because she and my father both came from Lexington, Virginia, though they only met when we were in Shanghai. The last time we had seen her was just before we left China in 1940.

When she came to visit us in Charles Town, West Virginia, nine years later, her round face was as wrinkled as a dried apple and she was almost toothless. Her hair, peeking out from under her deaconess headdress, was white, and when she took off the headdress it barely covered her pink scalp.There are two things she said that I have remembered all my life. One was said as she was smacking her lips over some particularly delicious dessert my mother had made: "I've only got one tooth left, but it's all right. The dentist says it's my sweet one." The other: "I was the last person Robert E. Lee kissed before he died, and now I have kissed you."

There is, of course, a lifetime between that second sentence and the first, and although the last time I saw Maud she was eighty and I was sixteen, it is now that I am over eighty myself that I have been able to fill in those long decades between. As I mentioned earlier, Kate DiCamillo was fascinated by the story of the famous kiss and told me if I didn't write about Maud, she would. But Maud was *my* hero, so I set about to find out more than the little I could remember from knowing her and hearing my parents talk about her. To my amazed delight, I found that her niece had donated many of her letters from China to the University of North Carolina and that there were a few letters from and about her in the Archives of the Episcopal Church. So over the course of a couple of years, I gave myself the task of putting together her life story. It's not part of my family history, but it touches it, first in Lexington, then Charles Town and Winchester (where my parents lived for thirty years), and, most importantly, in China.

Maud was born in Lexington, Virginia, on the 4th of December in 1868—three and a half years after Appomattox, the daughter of Mary and Francis William Henderson. She had, in the words of the Psalmist, a goodly heritage. Her father's two given names came from his two godfathers, Francis Scott Key (who wrote our national anthem) and Episcopal Bishop William Meade of the Virginia diocese and the son of one of Washington's aides. Francis Henderson was commissioned an officer in the US Army when Polk was president and was appointed the first postmaster in San Francisco. In 1861, he left the US Army and became a captain in the Confederate army, and, although he was a lawyer by the time Maud was born, he was always called "Captain Henderson."

The Hendersons were a military family. Francis Henderson's father was an army surgeon who, reportedly, made his rounds with his cat sitting on the pummel of his saddle. On the anniversary of his death, his widow told the family that she had something to do. She arranged her treasured articles, putting the names of each person who was to receive each item with the item, and then, in Maud's words, "fell asleep and did not wake this side."

The young Maud became too well acquainted with those who did not "wake this side." It began with her mother's death when Maud was a year and a half old. She had a remarkable memory.

She remembered her father carrying her in to see her mother, hoping his wife would rouse enough to see her only living child. Her mother opened her eyes, Maud recalled. She was to die on Midsummer's Eve.

Maud also remembered, or perhaps was told of, a sweltering Sunday later that summer when she was sitting beside her father in the church pew. After she had marched animal crackers up and down the prayer book, she settled in for a morning nap. Later, on the porch at the home of their friends the Lees, it was revealed that Maud was not the only napper that morning. She was occupying her accustomed spot on the general's lap when he asked her, "What do you think of a daughter who pokes her father in the ribs with her elbow when he is nodding his approval of the preacher's sermon?"

The storied Southern general was a close friend of her father's and made a particular pet of little Maud. Traveller, the horse who had carried Lee through the war, provided her first horseback ride. Then at the end of September 1870 came the evening of the famous kiss. Her father and the general had attended the vestry meeting together at the Episcopal church and Maud had been left in the care of Mrs. Lee and their daughter, Mildred. When the men returned, the general carried Maud through the kitchen and took a cookie from the jar that stood in the pantry to give to Maud. Then he kissed her and handed her over to her father. She did not remember—but knew from being told—that her father was summoned not long afterward to the Lees' home. After the general had bade Maud and her father good-bye, he went into the dining room, where his family and supper were waiting. He sat down, but as he began the grace, his voice faltered and he slumped over the table, paralyzed by a massive stroke. He died two weeks later. Mrs. Lee told Captain Henderson that little Maud must be told that while others had kissed the general after that, Maud was the last one he kissed.

She remembered being taken to see the general as he lay in state in the chapel of Washington College, of which he had been president since the end of the war. She thought how impressive her friend looked in his gray full dress uniform and wondered why he would not wake and take her up in his arms as he always did. Some years later, with no prompting, she pointed out to Mildred Lee just where the cookie jar had stood on that long-ago evening.

So there were two great losses in Maud's life before she turned two, but the next four years were happy ones. Her father was her constant companion and people remarked how droll they looked strolling about the Virginia Military Institute campus—the tall captain and his tiny lady, "the slowest couple on the quad." There weren't other children in her life, but she didn't feel the lack of them. The adults who were her neighbors doted on her, one even supplying a Christmas Eve Santa who, Maud always believed, had actually come down the chimney. Her cats, Moses, Aaron, and Jim, were her playmates, though she admits much later that they should have been addressed as Mrs. Moses, Mrs. Aaron, and Mrs. Jim. Jim was the favorite. She and Jim played endless games of hide-and-seek and at night Jim would sleep on Maud's bed.

Then at nearly six, she was taken away from her beloved home and father in Lexington and sent to Charles Town, West Virginia, to stay with relatives. She was given no explanation for this move. It might have been an economic one, for while she was gone, the family home was rented out. Maud herself looked back on the years between 1874 and 1882 as her years of exile. From the time she was nine until she was thirteen and a half she was enrolled in the Episcopal Female Institute in Winchester, Virginia, eighteen miles to the east of Charles Town.

There is very little record of those years. I've only found two stories from them. One was that she asked to be confirmed by the Bishop of Virginia soon after the move, already planning at the age of nine to tell children in China about Jesus. Then there is in her later letters an extended account of an experience from the summer she was thirteen.

"Just before I went to Lexington in June, a friend living at Harpers Ferry was married and I was somehow included in the picnic for wedding guests and spent the day on Loudon Heights. I suppose we had something besides view, you can take that for granted, but my memory is *the view*, such a wonderful one, on a perfect day. The crowd started downhill and I stood looking drinking it in. They called me, I answered and stood looking down the Potomac, across the fields, and off in the far distant shimmering line which they said was Chesapeake Bay. As I stood I had a Psychic. It was as if a clear promise was given me 'nothing will ever take it away, it is yours.' And it has been my joy and refreshing through so many viewless days, or when *no view* would have been welcome."

Her return to Lexington by coach was a joyful one. Her father warned her that all the cats but one had long ago disappeared, as the renters had disliked cats. Jim had been spotted in the neighborhood from time to time, but she was now a feral cat, and no one dared approach her.

Maud jumped out of the coach almost before it reached her front door and stood at the gate taking in the old familiar sights. Under the neighbors' house she spied a cat. She was sure it was Jim. Maud called to her. The cat stood still for a minute, listening, then she bounded through the lilac bush, across the grass, and jumped up on Maud's shoulder. As they entered the house, Jim ran ahead and leaped onto Maud's old bed, curling up contentedly as she had in the old days.

Maud was obviously a bright and vivacious young woman. She bragged years later that she had once led the ball at the Virginia Military Institute, but she remained coy about the cadet who had invited her.

Two years after Maud's happy return to the home she loved, her father remarried. His new wife was Maria Eliza Hamilton, the great-granddaughter of Alexander Hamilton, one of our nation's founding fathers. Maria was from Maud's account a wonderful stepmother to her husband's teenaged daughter. She was a highly educated woman and was happy to share her learning and the books she loved with her eager pupil. Then when Maud was seventeen, Maria gave Maud the gift she had always wanted, a sister. Maud felt as though she was a second mother to little Louise, especially since the baby's own mother was frail after the birth. Maria died when Louise was not quite a year old and Maud was eighteen. Meantime, Francis Henderson had become gravely ill.

On the last day of his life, he was too weak to hold Louise in his arms, but he asked Maud to bring the baby in to see him. "Oh," he said. "I had so looked forward to her walking." Maud carried her thirteen-month-old sister a few steps away and put her down on her feet. "Walk to Daddy," Maud said, and the baby threw out her arms and took the few steps across the space to her father's chair.

"Have I told you about that wonderful last evening?" Maud asked in a birthday letter to the grown Louise. "He was in coma and they wanted me to leave his bedside, but I would not . . . He became conscious of my presence and called the old pet name, Dear Little Heart." And then, "Just at the last minute his face was transformed with life and joy, and as he passed over to the other side he rapturously called: 'Mary, my mother, my Redeemer,'" as though, Maud thought, he was greeting Maud's mother, his own mother, and Jesus as he woke on the other side.

Although Maud was almost nineteen and had been caring for her sister since the child was born, on the death of her father, Maria's family came to claim the baby and take her to live with them in South Carolina. It was decided that her father's younger brother, Commodore Alexander Henderson, and his wife, Catherine, should adopt Maud and take her to live with them in Boston.

I do not know if Maud had met her famous uncle before she became his ward. More than distance had separated the two families. Commodore Henderson had entered the navy in 1851 and the following year, as a young officer, cruised the Far East with Commodore Perry. It was on that voyage in 1854 that Perry's fleet sailed into Tokyo Bay and caused the Japanese government to open its doors to the West.

The young naval engineer went on to serve in the Mediterranean and South Atlantic, and in 1861 when his Virginia brother Francis was joining the Confederate army, Alexander returned to the States and served with distinction in the Northern navy throughout the Civil War.

In 1882 when the United States began the task of building a "new navy," Alexander Henderson was made the engineering head of the Naval Advisory Board, designing the "new navy's" first vessels and supervising the building of them. When this work was done, he became the Chief Engineer of the Boston Navy Yard, where he was welcomed into Boston's elite society.

It was into this privileged household that Maud went in early 1888. We can only imagine that she arrived in Boston, physically and psychically exhausted, having, over the last two years, almost single-handedly cared for her invalid parents and her baby sister.

She was now orphaned and bereft of the only member of her family still living, a toddler who would be likely to forget ever having known her.

Her Boston aunt and uncle seemed determined to help her enjoy life. At one dinner party she was seated next to the venerable Oliver Wendell Holmes, whose work she knew well, thanks to her stepmother's tutelage.

Referring to a passage in *Poet of the Breakfast Table,* Maud said something to the effect that she understood that there was one path across Boston Commons that a young man must not ask a young woman to take unless he meant business. Which path was that? she asked Holmes.

"Ah," she remembered the elderly doctor saying, "if I were only fifty years younger I would show you."

But the life of luxury was not for Maud. Less than two years later she entered the Boston City Hospital Training School for Nurses, and after graduation went as a nurse to Hanover, New Hampshire, to what was known then as Mary Hitchcock Hospital. She made a lifelong friend there—this much I do know because in one of her letters from China, she reminds her friend of their climbing a New Hampshire mountain that reminded her of her "psychic" experience in West Virginia.

The Spanish-American War interrupted her time in Hanover and she became for the duration head of the camp hospital at Montauk Point, Long Island. She was barely thirty, but despite her youth and tiny height must have become a figure to be reckoned with. With the end of the war, she turned once again to her childhood dream of telling Chinese children about Jesus and enrolled in the Episcopal Church's training school for deaconesses in New York City. Maud was ordained as a deaconess in 1903 and then set out for China. She was not to see her native land again for forty-three years.

The picture of Maud in the 1903 class of deaconesses shows a serious, determined face—the face of a young woman ready to take charge, and in her early letters from China, she is doing just that. But she had a run-in with an Episcopal bishop who wanted to house former prostitutes in her school for girls, and after briefly joining another mission where she was considered too liberal for their liking, she decided to go out on her own.

Many female babies were abandoned in those days, and Maud was determined to give abandoned girls a home when they had none, providing them with schooling and the skills to make a living and, when the time came, arranging for a good marriage. St. Faith's, as she called her compound, was financed entirely by donations, some from friends abroad and some from admiring Chinese benefactors.

Over the years hundreds of babies and girls would call Maud "Mother" or "Grandmother." Her letters, mostly to her half sister, Louise, whom she hadn't seen since Louise was a tiny child, tell of the joys and hardships of life behind the walls of St. Faith's. There was the occasion when a tiny blister on her finger turned into a blood infection that nearly took her life. The Episcopal

Mission doctor suggested gently that if she had anything she wished to attend to she should do it at once, for "I think tomorrow you will be too weak."

Maud with one of her many children.

"In an instant," Maud wrote, "flashed into my mind my father's last words, 'Mary, my mother, my Redeemer.'" Despite the fact that she had parted ways with the Episcopal Mission years before, the Bishop of Shanghai, who was ill, sent the mission treasurer to help her put her financial affairs in order, and a priest came to have Communion with her and talk about where she wished to be buried. But Maud, crediting much prayer and good doctors, survived to continue her life with her children at St. Faith's.

There were no easy times during Maud's years at St. Faith's. There was a worldwide depression, so funds were always scarce. China was in perpetual political turmoil. Although the nation became a republic in 1912 under Sun Yat-sen, there continued to be struggles among various local warlords and the rising Communist party. Shanghai was an international city—part of it a French concession and another the so-called International Concession, which included former British and American concessions. The Municipal Councils in these areas excluded Chinese members, and the police and civil servants were foreigners. Even the names of the streets reflected foreign imperialism—such as Jessfield Road, on which St. Faith's was located.

The international presence offered a certain degree of safety for foreign residents until 1937, when the Sino-Japanese War began. At this point refugees poured into the city. Those who had grown up in St. Faith's came home and the compound was full to overflowing. The final straw that winter occurred when thieves broke in and stole everything from a Christmas gift of beef to rice, beans, and utensils.

"Bombs, rumours, refugees, measles, simultaneously. One day in the thick of it Grandma [as everyone including Maud herself called her] exclaimed, 'Where's the fun?' . . . [The answer came from the group] 'On Grandma's face!' Yes, Grandma saw the joke. She had asked the question in fun and they had seen the joke.

"Grandma once lost her sense of humor—my daddy had long ago charged me never to lose it because any one finding it might have such a hard time. Well I knew I was up against it because I had lost my sense of humour, and was weeping for it! Will I ever live to see how funny it is to cry for your sense of humour and as the thought came, the rainbow shone through. My sense of humour was welcomed back with a hearty chuckle."

August, 1938:

"Here we are at it again. Glory [gory] thrust upon us. Now on to Sept. Your New York papers today will be telling you that things are easing up a bit around Shanghai for now. . . For some days I was busy receiving and fixing up refugees. 'Boy'—faithful helper for over a quarter of a century—was off in the Chinese soldier zone collecting his wife and son and little daughter. One little one already here. I was listening to every knock on the door hoping it was their arrival. They arrived after a trying detour safe and sound. Once, I was opening the door, as I thought for his family, one of 'my girls' of twenty-seven years ago was standing there asking if she could come in—'Come home to Grandma?' One baby in her arms, another yet unborn, and three daughters and a son. They had walked miles, such a detour. Nothing but the one outfit of clothing they wore. The father too was there. Of course they came in. They were so worn and tired. Roadside food was scarce these days.

"As I write the airplanes are droning overhead, just overhead. One never knows what may happen—by accident or malice prepense. Shrapnel meant for another airplane fell on the roof, close by me in the court where I was standing with several members of the family. Roof tiles were broken and thrown aside. The hot piece lay smoking on the roof, and on touching broke into four pieces. I am not an enthusiast about collecting red-hot war trophies, but I

150

am treasuring these bits. No one was hurt. If the largest, if either, had struck us we would not now be telling you about it. The boom of cannon and anti-aircraft fire has been quieter these last few days, and the noise of the machine guns. And I sleep wonderfully well—truly. And with this great family for every reason I must keep everything as normal as possible. Kindergarten, grade school and sewing hours, prayer time as usual though for 143 big and little I stand looking on, encouraging to quietness, the kindergarten songs are punctured by the boom of cannon.

"Age seventy (Chinese count [in China everyone becomes a year older on New Year's Day]), temperature hovering around in the nineties 85.6 yesterday, hotter today. One of my former pupils, an orphan boy is living here and working in the Stadium, adapted as a soldiers' hospital and full of the wounded, quite nearby. Another 'child,' pupil once, then teacher, goes to another hospital for night duty tonight. We are in the thick of it."

There was no mail going out in those days, so the letter begun in August is continued in September and is still being written in November.

"September 6th. Pretty busy. Yesterday the temperature was 97.7 in the shade and plenty moist. Today about the same. In the meantime things are pretty lively, in and out . . . Today when the new land-lord, with his eviction bombs was serving his notice on the many years lord of the land, the Great Land Lord staged a thunderstorm. Such an afternoon—which was which? As I went my rounds, looking after [chores] and folks I found my silly brain saying over a rhyme that Mary Hunter used to say in the old days long ago:

'Charlotte, when she saw his body
Carried by her on a shutter,
Like a well conducted person
Went on cutting bread and butter.'

"One has to 'go on cutting bread and butter.' I found myself seeing the old dining room at 85 State and the group around the table and smiling with them. . . . The food problem is not an easy one. Last week we were reduced to one egg. It was boiled for me for my breakfast, but I voted it to the nurse who was going out to be with the wounded soldiers . . ."

As terrifying as the period of bombing was, the time of occupation was worse. St. Faith's was located on Jessfield Road next door to Japanese headquarters. Maud did not dare let any of her girls out of the gate for fear that they might be raped and even killed. She related with horror stories of twenty-four young women who answered ads for office jobs only to be locked in and their clothes taken away. Twenty-three were never heard from again. The twenty-fourth managed to obtain clothes of a Japanese man and somehow made her way home. Her parents, overjoyed to see her, were nevertheless concerned for her haggard appearance and, of course, begged to know where she had been and what she had been doing. "Oh," she said. "I've been a little unwell and could not come. Now please just let me go to bed." She went into her room and wrote a note detailing the horrors she had endured and committed suicide. "I still pray," Maud said, "for strength to carry on, until this tyranny is passed."

Marian Craighill, the wife of the Episcopal Bishop of Anking, told of visiting Maud in May of 1938. "Last Sunday afternoon Alma and I made an interesting call on Deaconess Henderson . . . I had heard a lot of how she lived absolutely like the Chinese around her and how she shared her bedroom with the babies and how she did everything for the orphans who came to her—your only credential seemed to be that of need. I went as far as the door with Pearl Buck in 1927 to see if she would take in her amah's unborn child if it turned out to be a girl—and she had the only place that would, Pearl said. . . . With this introduction you can see my real curiosity as we pounded on the wooden gate in a narrow crowded alley off from Jessfield Road. At first we thought we would pound in vain, but finally we heard a voice and through the chinks we saw Miss Henderson, rattling with keys. As she opened the gate she asked us if we thought we could get in, for the courtyard was flooded and we had to crawl along benches. Right in front of us was the main room of the Chinese house she lives in, simply full of recumbent figures of young girls, taking their afternoon rest. They were covering every inch of space, and the wooden affairs they were lying on proved later to be their desks and benches, and still later their dining tables when they brought in a kind of orange peel tea as we were leaving. . . . They were all of them her old children, who had returned to her when the Japanese drove them out . . . [T]he thing that struck horror to my soul was that they are next door to Japanese headquarters, and she doesn't dare let the Japanese know of the existence of these girls, so they literally never go out."

After describing Maud's own crowded bedroom with its faded pictures of the Lee family on her wall, Mrs. Craighill described Maud as "71 years old, dressed in an ancient Chinese type garment, with the charm of manner and the lovely voice of a cultured gentlewoman of Virginia." [*The Craighills of China*, Marian G. Craighill, Trinity Press, 1972, from pp. 221–223.]

After Pearl Harbor on December 7, 1941, there are no letters from Jessfield Road. As I said earlier, my parents told me a story they had heard from someone, that when at last the soldiers came to take Maud's girls, she stood in the doorway and said they would have to kill her first. Whatever the truth of that account, it is true that she was somehow able to stay on at St. Faith's long after most foreign nationals had been taken to detention camps. She was finally interned, sometime in 1944. Sadly, I do not know what became of her beloved children and grandchildren when she was no longer there to care for them and protect them.

After the war ended, there was a flurry of correspondence among various persons in China and the United States, trying to figure out exactly what to do with Maud Henderson. St. Faith's no longer existed and she was too old to start all over again. She was not the responsibility of the Episcopal Mission, having left its jurisdiction. She yearned to go "home" to Lexington, but the people who knew and loved her there were long dead, and their surviving children could not imagine what they would do if the elderly Maud should land on their doorsteps. Strangely, there are no letters from her half sister and her family. The only relative that stepped up was Thomas Hale, who was the husband of her cousin Elizabeth, the commodore's daughter. In 1946, he arranged for her passage back to America and several stops along the way, though letters from her hosts seem less than gracious, asking, for example, that they be reimbursed for the cost of housing Maud for a couple of days. She had a visit to Lexington and was interviewed at length by the local newspaper. In the article she expressed her joy to be in the place that she so loved as a girl, but there was no permanent welcome there. It was finally agreed that she should have a place in the Episcopal Home in Richmond. It was from Richmond that she went to see her old friend in Hanover, New Hampshire, and later came to visit our family and revisit haunts of her childhood in Charles Town and Winchester.

It makes me sad to know that there were not many happy times after that. She began to decline physically and mentally and finally died in 1956 at the age of eighty-five.

The newspaper accounts of her return after forty-three years in China tell of the old lady I remember, recalling her special relation to General Lee and his family, bragging that she got respect from the commander of the Japanese detention camp when she told him that her uncle had sailed into Tokyo Bay with Commodore Perry.

"After her fruitless search for General Lee's portrait in Commodore Henderson's old sea chest," a *Richmond Times-Dispatch* reporter relates, "Miss Henderson walked over to her bedroom mirror. Dozens of snapshots of members of her Chinese family are stuck around the edges of the mirror.

"She identified some of them. This one married a minister. That one became a Red Cross worker. Another lost the sight of one eye, but the doctors saved the sight of the other.

"'Sometimes I get homesick for China,' Miss Henderson confessed."

When the reporter asked her to point to her most satisfying memory of those years, she recalled a time when anti-foreign feeling was running high in Shanghai. A Chinese boy approached her outside her door, pointed, and yelled: "She is a foreigner! She is a foreigner!"

But her own children shouted back: "She is no foreigner. She is the grandmother who belongs here."

And there is a letter she kept. It is undated, but was probably received in 1950.

My dearest Friend,

As I am urging our students to write a note to their mothers away from Shanghai, I think of you as a mother to so many of our Chinese girls. The greatness and depth of your love only God knows how to measure and reward you. Thinking of you has always been an inspiration to me. I love you.

Lovingly yours,
Tszo-Sing Chen

She was proud to have been kissed by Robert E. Lee. I am proud to have been kissed by Maud Henderson.

I can't resist adding a family story here. After my mother died, my father insisted on moving to a retirement home despite the fact that we had bought a house with a first-floor room and bath so he could live with us. "Then you'd want to go somewhere, and you'd say, 'What will we do with poor old Pop?'" At the retirement home was a woman who took a great shine to Daddy, but whose dementia made her a bit intimidating to the rest of the residents. So when he died, everyone was afraid to break the news to her. But when someone finally did, she said: "Oh, that Mr. Womeldorf. He was such a gentleman. He'd make Robert E. Lee look like a hobo." My regret when I heard that story was that I couldn't share it with my father. He would have gotten such a laugh from it.

Note: Many of Maud Henderson's letters from China can be found in the Archives of the Library of the University of North Carolina. I am also indebted to The Episcopal Historical Society for other correspondence.

Suzy, Clava, and me at the Lovettsville reunion.

The Teaching Life

The year after that visit from Maud Henderson, I graduated from high school and went on to spend four years getting my degree in English literature from King College in Bristol, Tennessee. I decided during my last year of college to take a year out from studying. I would teach school, thought I. I'd taken an education course or two and done a stint of practice teaching to have something to go with my English major that even then, no one considered practical, but which for me was life changing, thanks to

158

the brilliant, caring professors who introduced me to great ideas and great writers. Gilly Hopkins, more than incidentally, takes her surname from Gerard Manley Hopkins, the subject of my senior thesis.

There were some requests for teachers posted on the bulletin board that were in school districts fairly close to where my parents were living, so I made inquiries. One school in Lovettsville, Virginia, noted that their long-time principal was named Womeldorph. Although Mr. Womeldorph was retiring and spelled his name with a *ph* rather than an *f*, it seemed like a sign of sorts, so I applied to become the sixth-grade teacher for the enormous salary of five thousand dollars a year.

The population of Lovettsville was 340 (according to the sign on the edge of town), but students were bused into the elementary school from the rural areas of upper Loudon County. This part of Loudon County became famous a few years later because it was featured in a documentary on hunger in America. The southern part of the county was mostly horse farms for millionaires. Several of the Kennedys owned property there. But people in lower Loudon County didn't send their children to public schools, and there was no appetite for taxing the rich county southerners to help the less fortunate northerners.

The Lovettsville Elementary School was an old brick building from another era. There was an auditorium of sorts, but no library in the school, no lunchroom, and no gym. Everything except outdoor recess would take place in my classroom. There was no music teacher, no art teacher, no playground aid. I would be in charge of everything those children would get in the way of schooling, indoors or out.

Single teachers, I was told, always boarded with a couple who lived a short distance down the street from the school. The second-grade teacher, who was also just out of college, and I roomed there together. Our landlady was a kind person that both of us got along with. Her husband was another matter. For the only time in my life I would be living with a chain-smoking semi-invalid whose chief point of pride in life was his membership in the Ku Klux Clan. Fortunately, I escaped every weekend and went to Winchester to stay with my folks. Sometimes I would take Eleanor along, just to give her a break from the boarding house environment.

Mr. Myers, the new principal, showed me my classroom. It was in the basement—the only room down there besides the bathrooms and the furnace room. There were windows along one side and, in the hall, a door that opened onto the playground. The classroom was crowded with battered, carved-up desks because there would be thirty-six sixth graders in the class, and they ranged from one who was the age of ten, to three who were sixteen. The long-time third-grade teacher was famous for holding children back for multiple reappearances in her class.

I didn't know what to expect of such an assortment of kids. It didn't help that the first introduction I had was a paper listing their IQ scores. I was appalled. How was I with no real experience supposed to teach children with such a difference in their ages, a frightening number of whom had IQ scores in the low 70s? I stopped reading and just stuck the records out of sight in a bottom drawer of my desk, and never thought of them again until the end of the year when I was throwing away the accumulation of papers in my desk. I was furious with those scores. My kids were not dumb! I've never trusted standardized tests since.

School opened and they came, the real children, not the ones on paper. By the end of the first week or so I was in love with them all, even Junior, who heartily hated school and was absent as often as he was present, and Godfrey, who was such a creative misbehaviorist, no one could have disliked him.

I don't know what any of them gained academically from being in that basement room. I know I wasn't much of a teacher, but we had some great times. What I lacked in pedagogical skill, I made up for by reading aloud—everything from *The Lion, the Witch and the Wardrobe* and *Huckleberry Finn* to Shakespeare. *Macbeth* was a class favorite—all that gore. I'm sure I skipped and explained our way through several pages of the play, but they had a taste of greatness, anyhow.

On rainy days, we'd push back all the desks and do broad jumping in the cleared space. Mr. Myers poked his head in one day, but just grinned and went on back upstairs.

Even though they lived just over an hour from Washington, DC, most of the class had never visited the capital. I racked my brain to figure out a curriculum-related excuse to take them all

"This is your life, Miss Womeldorf."
Lovettsville School, 1955.

The Lovettsville class reunion crowd.

there. We were doing ancient world history, which hardly qualified, but then I realized our nation's capital held a re-creation of early Roman catacombs as well as a European-style cathedral. They would be the educational excuse. My hidden agenda was the National Zoo.

This was the spring of 1955. Today, not only would such a trip be impossible, any teacher who tried to do what I did that day would be fired on the spot. Other than the bus driver, I was the single adult on the trip. Junior was playing hooky again, so there were thirty-five children. We all hung out the windows staring at the monuments as we crossed the bridge into the city, but there was no time to stop and see them. We visited the fake catacombs and hurried through the cathedral, but by the time we got to the zoo, there was less than an hour left before we'd have to leave. The bus driver had to get back to drive his afternoon route. He told me more than once that the bus was leaving at two p.m. Anyone not on it would be left behind.

There were more wonderful creatures to see in the zoo than there were children to see them. Everyone was excited and eager to head off. How could I make them walk around in lockstep like little Madeleine schoolgirls for fifty minutes? They'd explode. We were standing near a sign with arrows indicating all the various exhibits. There was a large clock nearby. I pointed to it. "You can take your lunch and follow the arrows to anything you want to see, but at ten minutes before two, you have got to be lined up right here, ready to get back on the bus. If

163

you're late, the driver says he'll leave you behind."

I stood there and watched thirty-five children disappear in almost as many different directions and was suddenly horrified by what I'd done. *What if someone got lost or hurt? Suppose they didn't come back on time? What would I do then?* For fifty minutes I simply sat on a bench near the clock becoming more anxious by the minute. Every now and then in the distance I'd hear a happy shout from a voice I recognized. The children were having fun, but I certainly wasn't. I must have been out of my mind. Then, miraculously, just before 2:50, I saw them come running from every direction. They lined up before me two by two and at exactly 2:50, I counted heads. I had thirty-four happy children standing exactly where they should. I was one short.

"Has anyone seen Godfrey?" I asked, trying hard not to panic. At that moment, a grinning Godfrey stepped out from behind a large tree and took his place at the end of the line. Everyone was on time, except the bus driver, that is. He didn't appear until five after two. But we got back to school on time. No one told on their irresponsible teacher. All was well.

Some years ago I had a phone call from out of the blue. It was Clara Washington, one of my Lovettsville sixth graders of years before. She was a grandmother now. She had read my books to her children and was now reading them to her grandchildren. Curious about the author, she went to my website and learned to her delight that I had been Miss Womeldorf, her sixth-grade teacher. Clara wanted to arrange a reunion of the class. If she did, would I come? "Name the day," I said. Eleven of the thirty-six came with various spouses and children. And those there gave me news of several of the others who weren't. Junior was now the owner of a successful trash-hauling business. Godfrey had come back from Vietnam but not really home. He spent most of his time in the woods alone. Someone had seen him in town and told him about the reunion. He had said he might come, but to my sorrow, he didn't.

I'd taken the little album into which I'd pasted their school pictures and pictures of the surprise farewell party they'd given me at the end of the year.

"I can't believe you kept our pictures," Suzy said.

"I can believe I kept them," I said. "I can't believe that I was able to find them."

A few years before the reunion, I was driving from Dulles Airport to a high school reunion in Charles Town when I saw a sign pointing toward Lovettsville. On an impulse, I drove there. I hadn't seen the school or the town since I'd left in 1955. The old building was now a community center. I was directed to the new one. It was June and school was just over for the year. I stopped at the office, as visitors always have to these days. "I taught in the old school many years ago," I said to the secretary. "Would it be all right if I just looked around?"

She told me that it was the last day for the staff, so they were all busy, but she didn't think they'd mind if I looked around. It was a beautiful new school, the kind that I wished I could have given my sixth graders. The center of the building was a large library where the librarian was sitting on the floor shelving books. She looked up when I came in. It was evident that she was hot and tired and not at all eager to entertain a visitor. I apologized but told her that I'd taught in the old school where the only library was the collection of books I'd brought from home to put in my classroom. I was so thrilled to see that the children of Lovettsville now had this great library.

She asked me what my name was. "Back then, I was Katherine Womeldorf," I said. "I'm Katherine Paterson now."

"You're kidding," she said. "Not Katherine Paterson the writer."

I admitted that I was.

"You have made my day," she said, and got up from the floor to shake my hand. Then she sent someone to summon all the teachers in the building. I had a great time answering their questions, hearing about life in Lovettsville today, signing the library's collection of my books. There were even teachers who remembered some of the teachers I had taught with more than thirty years before.

The young man who was the current sixth-grade teacher said: "Every year when we read *Bridge to Terabithia* I tell my students that Lovettsville is Lark Creek, and they never believe me."

I assured him that he was right.

His face lit up with a triumphant smile. "Now they'll *have* to believe me," he said.

166

One of the most useful bits of advice for beginning teachers was given to me by an ex-teacher during my last year in college. She had heard that I was planning to teach the following year. "You're very young looking," she said. "And sometimes children take advantage of young teachers, so I want to pass along the most helpful advice I was given when I was a young teacher. This is it. When you begin to feel a slight rumbling in the class that you sense is going to build, stand up in front. Don't say anything. Just think as hard as you can: 'If you don't sit down and shut up I'm going to beat the living daylights out of you.' Remember, don't say a word. You'll ruin it if you say anything." I can't recall ever having to use this advice in Lovettsville. But the time would come.

It wasn't until eight years later, in 1963, that I found myself a classroom teacher again. John and I had been married a year when he decided to pursue a graduate degree at Princeton Theological Seminary. He quickly found a part-time job at the large Presbyterian church that abuts the Princeton University campus, but I would need a full-time job if we were going to make ends meet. The State of New Jersey was less than impressed with my sparse college credits in education or my single year in a school in rural Virginia, so there was no hope that I could teach in a public school.

I learned somehow of an opening at a boys' prep school a few miles away. They needed someone who could teach the eleventh- and twelfth-grade Sacred Studies, a required course in this Methodist school, and seventh-grade English. By this time I had had three years of theological training and I had majored in English, so it looked like the ideal job.

In late August the headmaster invited me over for an interview. He was a large, imposing former District Superintendent of the Methodist Church. He assured me that on paper I was well qualified for the position, but he needed to explain that the boys had been so cruel to the last Sacred Studies Master, that he had fled before the semester was over. He looked at me closely over his wide desk. "Do you think you can manage it?"

"I'll try," I said a bit shakily.

He slammed his fist on the desk. "Trying won't do it! It's sink or swim."

I needed the job, so I agreed to take it.

"Oh, by the way," I said, "what textbook do you use?"

"The Bible," he said as though that should be self-evident.

By November we worked our way from Genesis through the Patriarchs and Judges, past David and Solomon and into the troubled history of the divided Kingdoms of Judah and Israel. The boys mostly behaved, but it was clear that they felt the study of the Bible was useless and I should therefore be passing out easy A's simply for their willingness to sit through class. On that particular day, we had gotten as far as the last days of the Kingdom of Israel, which consists of the assassination of one king after another until the country is ripe for the Assyrian conquest.

Someone pointed out for the umpteenth time how foolish

those people were, they did nothing but kill off their kings. Why, when there were so many important things to learn, were they wasting their time studying this stuff?

Before I could answer, the door to the classroom was thrown open. The history master was standing in the doorway, ashen faced. "The president has been shot," he said.

Without a word, we filed out into the common area where there was a large television set and watched in horror until Walter Cronkite finally announced the news that Kennedy was dead. The boys didn't try to argue about the stupidity of the ancient Hebrews again.

When I had to tell the headmaster that I was expecting a baby, I was sure he'd dismiss me. If I had been a public school teacher in New Jersey in those days, I would have had to resign. But the headmaster thought it would be good for the boys and told me I should teach as long as I felt up to it. I finished the year. Two weeks later, John Jr. was born. To the boys' credit, they were terrific, almost gallant, in their concern for their pregnant "master."

I was the only full-time woman on the faculty, but there was one other woman, the drama teacher who came in several mornings a week. At the end of the year she confessed that whenever she was in the building during the first few weeks of school she had stood outside my classroom. She wanted someone to be there for me when I came running out crying. But I never did. Knowing full well what had happened the previous year, she finally said to one of the students: "Mrs. Paterson seems to be doing all right. Is everybody behaving for her?"

"Oh, yeah," the boy said. "We don't dare do anything. She has this *look*."

Me in a kimono.

Japan Days

When I tell people what I was doing in the years 1957–1961, most of them are visibly shocked. It seems in this day and age it would be more forgivable to say you were once a prostitute than to reveal the fact that you were once a Christian missionary. I've been asked point-blank: "What right do you have to force other people to accept your religion?" The easy answer to that is, of course, that it is impossible to force another person to accept any idea, secular or religious. I suppose the conquistadores could threaten a population with death if they didn't accept baptism, but even that didn't guarantee a change of heart or mind

And actually, during the four years I spent in Japan, the heart and mind that changed the most was my own. As a child, I hated and feared the Japanese—they were the enemy, and if anyone had told me when I was nine that someday I would go to live in Japan, I would never have believed him. The Japanese had bombed and devastated China. The conquering army had perpetrated untold atrocities. The Japanese had occupied my home and twice forced us to leave the land I loved.

In the fall of 1941, we settled in Winston-Salem, North Carolina, where my father's assignment was to start a new church out from the center of town. Before there was any church building Daddy led Sunday afternoon services in the home of a family in the community. That particular Sunday afternoon the phone rang in the middle of the service. Mr. Taylor left the room to answer it, and minutes later appeared at the doorway, visibly shaken. "The Japanese have bombed Pearl Harbor," he said. I still remember the terror I felt. The invasion the soldiers had promised my father in Tsing Tao had begun. It was the end of everything.

I'm sure I was only one of the millions of American children who played commandos, collected scrap, and spent much of my meager allowance on war savings stamps. But I did it with a fervor none of my classmates shared. I had actually seen the enemy face-to-face. I knew they had to be defeated before they invaded San Francisco.

When I entered graduate school to train for missionary service, I expected to go to Taiwan, which was as close to my beloved China as it was possible to be in the mid-fifties. But when I went for my interview with the mission board, it became clear that Taiwan would not be a possibility. Back in Richmond, I had a Japanese friend, Ai Kuroki, who somehow persuaded me that if I gave the Japanese people a chance I would come to love them. I loved and respected Ai, so the summer after graduation I went to the training program for new Southern Presbyterian missionaries in Montreat, North Carolina, to prepare for work in Japan.

One of the instructors was a linguist whose job it was to help us hear and repeat the sounds peculiar to the languages we would have to learn to work in our chosen countries. A colleague of hers had discovered that the Biblical sentence found in John 4:7 contained all the sounds in nearly every known language. So whether the nascent missionary was going to Brazil or Mexico or Congo or Taiwan or Korea or Japan, we all memorized this particular sentence: "A Samaritan woman came to draw water." The Japanese Bible had skipped the word *Samaritan* and translated the sentence so it read roughly: "A certain woman came to draw water." Which after more than fifty years I remember as: *Are no onna no hito wa mizu o tori ni kimashita.* I'm sure the well-rehearsed sentence helped me learn how to hear and pronounce Japanese when I finally got to language school three months later, but otherwise it wasn't a great deal of help. I mean, how often could you work this, your one beautifully memorized sentence, into a conversation?

It was put to the test my first day in Japan. The freighter on which I traveled docked in Yokohama before proceeding on to Kobe, which was my destination. We had the day free while the ship unloaded cargo, and I was determined to go into Tokyo and see my friend Ai Kuroki. I'd had no way of letting her know when I would get to Japan or if I'd even have a chance to stop in Tokyo, but I had her address. I'd just go and surprise her. A shipmate who heard I was going to Tokyo asked if she could go with me. Somehow we changed some dollars into yen and found a tiny taxi to carry us into the big city. And big it was. During the war, hardly anyone studied English, and the only Japanese I knew concerned a certain Samaritan woman of questionable morals, so asking directions became more than a challenge. We somehow found our way to a police box located in the neighborhood designated by Ai's address. I didn't realize that what I had in my hand wasn't really a street address with a house number, it was a block address. Some kindly neighbor walked by as the baffled policeman tried to figure out who we were and what we wanted. She motioned for us to follow her and led us to a house, pointed at it, smiled, nodded, and went on her way.

I opened the sliding door, stepped into the little vestibule, and called Ai's name. At first there was no answer at all. Then at last an elderly woman came shuffling out of the house and knelt on the edge of the tatami. She looked at us and said something which, for all I knew, was "What on earth?" I bowed as low as I could, but all I could say in Japanese beyond *thank you, good-bye,* and *good afternoon* was: *Are no onna no hito wa* etc. It seemed wiser to stick to English. I showed her the address with Ai's name on it, but it was obvious that English was not her second, third, or any number language. Nevertheless, she shyly gestured for us to come on into the house. We had enough sense at least to leave our shoes behind in the vestibule before we stepped up and followed her into a large, mostly bare tatami-matted room and sat on the cushions she spread out for us. Then she disappeared. Minutes passed. Many minutes. There was no sound in the house at all except perhaps for our own heavy breathing. Finally I got up and began to wander around. I didn't even know if we were in the right house. But on sneaking into an adjourning room I spied a group photograph. On close examination, I found Ai's familiar face.

I raced back to whisper the good news to my friend and sat down again to wait some more. Finally, the little woman came back and gestured to me to follow her. She had already brought my shoes around to the back door. We went out of the house and into the house of a neighbor, where a telephone was handed to me. At the other end I heard Ai's voice, warm and welcoming. She was at the school where she taught, but she would come and get us as soon as she could because some of her students were arranging entertainment for us and then, if we had time, we would go to dinner. Meantime her mother would take care of us. Ah, of course, that was who our elderly hostess was. While we waited, Ai's mother served us tea and chatted on about something we naturally could not understand. When Ai arrived she took us in hand and gave us a wonderful evening. A group of her high school girls danced for us and I had my first Japanese meal, which I remember as delicious and beautifully arranged on a series of little plates and bowls. Already I was beginning to love Japan.

The next day we sailed for Kobe but we couldn't dock because a typhoon was predicted. We would have to ride the storm out farther from shore. All the passengers were anxious about the prospect. Well, at least my final day had turned out to be such a happy one. I went to my cabin and wrote a letter to my parents thanking them for all they had meant to me for the past nearly twenty-five years. How I thought a letter might survive when neither I nor the ship had, I don't know. But it seemed the thing to do. Then I went to bed and to sleep.

At breakfast the next morning I mentioned the fact that the typhoon had somehow bypassed us and was met with incredulity. "You slept through *that?*" Apparently, the other passengers had spent a terrified, sleepless night as gigantic waves rocked the freighter. I don't know what happened to my farewell letter, but I don't think I mailed it.

I spent the next two years in language school in Kobe. It was designed as a total immersion experience. Our teachers—all female except for the principal—were not allowed to speak English to us nor were we permitted to use English in the classroom. The best teachers were also the best mimes, acting out the meaning of new vocabulary words. Japanese is a difficult spoken language, as how you speak and even your vocabulary depends on who you are and to whom you are speaking.

Each day we went to school from nine to twelve. During the first hour the teacher reviewed with us the previous day's new lesson, helping us practice what we'd been introduced to. Sometimes, as we could understand more, the teacher would expound a bit on parts of the lesson so we'd better understand how to use what we'd learned. In the second hour, with another instructor, we were drilled on everything we'd learned so far, and in the third hour, yet another teacher introduced the day's new lesson. Along with our workbooks and vocabulary cards, we always carried home with us the admonition to practice, practice, practice.

Now, it happened that in the spring of my first year, I was given the opportunity to move into a beautiful Japanese house in the nearby city of Ashiya. The owner of the home was a widow of a prominent lawyer and because times were hard, she had taken in an American missionary friend of mine as a roomer. June was moving out of Mrs. Kimura's upstairs and suggested that I might like to take her place. "Mrs. Kimura will teach you so much that you'd never learn in language school," June said. "She has been the best teacher, both of language and customs, that I could imagine." I was thrilled by such a prospect. I had just lost my American roommate, so it was perfect timing for me. June made the introductions and it was agreed that I should come the following Friday, make the final arrangements with Mrs. Kimura, and move in a week later.

On the Friday morning before my visit, the new lesson contained a wonderful proverb. The literal translation of the original was "A professional would run away bare-footed." This saying, the teacher explained, had to do with an amateur who was so good that, seeing such excellence, the expert would be so embarrassed that he would forget his shoes at the door in his haste to retreat.

I practiced the proverb for the whole train ride to Ashiya. What greater compliment could I pay my future landlady than to tell her what a wonderful teacher she was, why, even those calling themselves teachers would rush away in haste before her excellence.

We inspected the gorgeous tatami-floored rooms upstairs, all four of which were to be mine. We visited the exquisite little garden and drank a cup of tea together. Finally after a wonderful hour or so, she saw me to the door, where I put on my shoes and thanked her again and said how very much I was looking forward to living in her house and learning from her. June had told me so much about what a wonderful teacher she was. "No, no," she protested, in a show of Japanese humility. "I'm no teacher." It was my perfect opening. "Oh, yes," I said, "a professional would run away bare-footed."

Her face seemed to go totally white. The atmosphere that had been all sunshine turned ice cold. Mrs. Kimura bowed briskly and abruptly disappeared into the house. Puzzled, I let myself out.

On Monday morning the first-hour teacher reviewed the lesson of Friday. "By the way," she said. "Don't ever use this proverb, especially never repeat it to a lady. It will sound as though you are calling her a prostitute."

I think I screamed. "Why didn't someone tell me this on Friday?" I was appalled. What should I do? Mrs. Kimura would never want me to cross her threshold again, much less let me live in her house for the next eighteen months. It was a nightmare. I was so proud of my great progress in the language and here I'd committed an unforgiveable faux pas to an elegant Japanese woman that I'd wanted so much to like me and mentor me. I finally called June and, though I didn't actually tell her what had happened, I asked her to find out if Mrs. Kimura was still expecting me to move in on Saturday.

She was. No mention was made by either of us of the previous week's visit when I came as planned and spent eighteen delightful months learning, as June had promised, much more than any school or text could teach me. For example, Mrs. Kimura would listen as I talked on the kitchen phone. "Excuse me for being rude and listening in on your phone conversation," she'd say, "but if you'd put it this way, it would be polite and people would understand you better." She was a devout Buddhist, but she would often conclude some hint on etiquette with the phrase: "You wouldn't want to embarrass Jesus, would you?"

When I left her home, which by then truly seemed to be our

home, she was distressed to see me go, especially since I was leaving her to go to the island of Shikoku that to her was like rural Mississippi is to a Manhattanite. "It'll ruin all the beautiful Japanese I've taught you," she mourned. "You'll come back speaking *Awa ben.*" Which is to say, like a hick. "But you must write me, you must practice your characters, and I'll mark them with red and send them back." So much for the woman who claimed not to be a teacher.

Just before I left for Shikoku I got up the nerve to ask her if she remembered that first visit and my terrible faux pas. She pretended, in true Japanese fashion, that it had never happened.

I had many amazing friendships during my four years in Japan. While I was still at language school in Kobe, a mutual acquaintance introduced me to Eiko Takahashi, a young woman not much older than I. Eiko spoke no English, and I was just learning Japanese. The war had robbed her of a high school education and she had endured a disastrous marriage and the loss of a child. We couldn't have been more different, but somehow, we quickly became friends. One day, quite out of the blue, she said to me, "For a long time I've been searching for a religion that would help me understand the meaning of my life, and I've never found one. I've often wondered about Christianity, but I haven't known how to find out about it. Would you mind if I went to church with you sometime?"

Now, you would think that I, the so-called missionary, might have been the one to first mention church, but I wasn't. As missionaries go, I, apparently, wasn't going very far very fast. But when Eiko asked for an invitation, I was happy to comply.

A couple of months later the pastor told me that Eiko had approached him and asked for baptism. I was shocked. "I don't want her to feel she has to become a Christian just because we're friends," I said.

He gave me what was very close to a withering look. "I think you can trust Eiko to make her own decision," he said. "She is quite ready to be baptized."

But baptism was only the first step for Eiko. She wanted to truly follow Jesus and she felt she could only do that by giving her life to serve others. She thought she needed more education to do that. So she studied for what would be the equivalent of a high school diploma and went on to get a degree in social work. It took her six or seven years, but she never gave up. And then after graduation, she went to a leper colony set on a tiny island in the Japan Sea and spent the rest of her life ministering to those despised by their families and their society. Like Maud Henderson, she has been one of the heroes of my life.

While I was in language school I had the chance to travel around Japan. The city of Nagoya is famous for its pottery. In a shop there I was looking at an array of truly elegant teacups. In the display was a misshapen cup about the color of mud. It seemed totally out of place in the shop, much less on that particular shelf. I couldn't resist lifting the lid, and gasped. The bottom of the lid was inlaid with gold. It was an experience that found its way into *Of Nightingales That Weep*. If you've read the book, you'll recall that Takiko sees a similar cup in a pottery shop and is puzzled until she lifts the lid. It reminds her of her stepfather, the potter, whose misshapen body repulsed her as a child.

In Osaka I got my first taste of Bunraku, Japanese puppetry that inspired *The Master Puppeteer*, and later, while I lived in Tokushima Province, I was able to meet the old artist who made puppet heads for the theater in Osaka.

I went to the island of Shikoku in the fall of 1959. My "bosses" were eleven Japanese pastors working in the mostly rural Tokushima Province. Over the course of a month or two I visited each church, staying in the pastors' homes, or if they were single, in the home of a parishioner. My own home was in the town of Komatsushima, right on the coast of the Japan Sea where the ferries from the main island of Honshu would dock and the nearby wharfs were crowded with the boats of fishermen. I lived in two rooms in a house on the edge of a huge rice paddy, going to sleep in spring and summer to the songs of thousands of frogs. My landlords belonged to Soka Gakkai, a radical Buddhist sect, well known for its intolerance of Christianity, but, as Mrs. Kuroda said, "Renting and religion are two different things." We lived together quite happily for two years. They never tried to convert me, but as I was leaving to return to the States, they did suggest that if I followed their example and chanted *namyo horenge kyo* morning, noon, and night, I might just find myself a husband in America.

There were no other Caucasians in my town, and if I really wanted to speak English, I needed to drive my little motorcycle ten miles down the road to Tokushima City, where there were two families from the Southern Presbyterian mission. There were English missionaries and a couple of American Roman Catholic priests in the area as well, but not many white faces.

In Komatsushima, Pastor Kosumi and his wife were my home away from home. Years later when my wonderful Japanese translator met Mrs. Kosumi, she said: "Kosumi San is your Japanese Maime Trotter, isn't she?" I'd never thought of Mrs. Kosumi, who hardly scraped my shoulder and weighed a few pounds more than my golden retriever, as Maime Trotter from *The Great Gilly Hopkins*, but when Hamae Okamoto said this, I realized how close she had come to the truth. Fusae Kosumi was also the kind of mother every child should have.

The nights I was in Komatsushima I nearly always ate dinner with the Kosumis. She was an amazing cook—the kind of cook that could go to anyone else's house, Japanese or foreign, and without asking for a recipe, go home and reproduce what she had tasted. On more than one occasion when I was watching her prepare a meal, she would gasp: *"Ara! Aka no!"* Which loosely translated means "Eek! No red!" and slip on her geta to race to the market to buy a carrot or red pepper to make the meal perfect. It was always important for the meal to look beautiful as well as taste good.

One night as she watched me happily devouring another

Eiko Takahashi.

Rev. and Mrs. Kosumi, who were my dearest friends in Komatsushima. She was the one my translator called my Japanese Maime Trotter.

A visit to the craftsman who made puppet heads for Bunraku. I didn't dream in 1960 I would be writing about Bunraku someday.

delicious meal, she remarked that I used chopsticks much better than her four children did. "But, then," she said, "when they were growing up during the war there was so little food for them to practice on." Bit by bit over the two years I was there, I learned about the war years when Christians were enemies of the state and merchants were told not to sell them food. Not that the Kosumis had money for food. Once, she said, she had sold her wedding kimono for two tomatoes.

In language school we had been urged to immerse ourselves in Japanese culture, so a friend and I went to a tea ceremony set up for tourists in a public park. We stood in line for some time before we were ushered into the tea house. All I remember about that experience was that the green tea was too bitter and the bean cakes too sweet. I was trying to understand the culture, but my reaction that day was "What's the big deal?" I didn't get the meaning, much less the value of the rite.

I was often on the road when I lived in Komatsushima, and after a longer than usual trip away, Mrs. Kosumi said to me, almost shyly: "I'd like to do tea for you to welcome you home." And in that humble house attached to a one-room tatami church, Mrs. Kosumi prepared the bitter green tea and sweet bean cakes. Lovingly and with enormous dignity, she went through the ancient ritual for which I was the only guest, and at last I understood.

The spring of my second year at language school I had been asked to come to the island of Shikoku and meet the pastors who were inviting me to join them in their work. As I stood in the long line waiting to buy my ticket to the ferry, I noticed an elderly woman with the milky white eyes of the blind. Before I could wonder how she could manage such a trip, a distinguished-looking older gentleman that I took to be her husband came back from where he'd gone to buy a box lunch and joined her in the line. I watched the couple for a long time, as the evident love and caring of the man for his wife was something I hadn't seen before in Japan, where women, especially wives, seemed to be second- or third-class citizens.

Once on the boat and almost before I could sit down, a group of very loud, very obnoxious, very drunk young men came rushing over to where I sat. In this society with a great tradition of the rules of etiquette, there were no rules in those days for how men should approach a young foreign woman traveling alone. It was assumed, somehow, that she was looking for adventure and these young men were determined to provide it for me.

I moved to another seat. They followed. This continued as I went up on deck, where, over the noise of the young men, I thought I heard singing. I moved toward the sound. To my amazement the music was that of a familiar hymn. I kept moving toward the music, my little band of drunken admirers surrounding me like a hoop skirt. When I got to the scene of the singing, I realized it was being led by the husband of the blind woman I'd seen in line. At the end of the next song, still surrounded by my unwelcome entourage, I went up to him. "I thought I heard you singing a Christian hymn," I said. He smiled and said they were.

He was a pastor in Wakimachi and he and some members of his church had gone to a meeting in Kobe and were now on the way home. "Wakimachi?" I exclaimed. "You are one of the pastors I'm on the way to meet."

I and my drunken crew joined the hymn sing. Me singing, my buddies looking on openmouthed. Before we got off the boat, one of the young men had cornered Pastor Iwaii to get the scoop on what he was all about.

Needless to say, over the next two years, Pastor Iwaii and I grew to be close friends. I went to Wakimachi every other month to teach a class on the Bible ostensibly to young people, but it proved to be the local entertainment for villagers of every age for whom a white face speaking Japanese was something of a marvel or perhaps a feature in a freak show.

When it was time for me to return to America, for what I thought would be a one-year leave, all eleven churches gave me a farewell party, but it is the party in Wakimachi that I remember the best.

In his message, Pastor Iwaii first read a verse in the Book of Ephesians that reads: "For [Christ] is our peace, who has made us both one, and has broken down the dividing wall of hostility." And the verse in Galatians in which the Apostle Paul says to the church: "There is neither Jew nor Greek, there is neither slave nor free, there is neither male nor female, for you are all one in Christ."

"Katherine," he said, "is young. I am old. She is a woman. I am a man. She is an American. I am Japanese. When she was the child of missionaries in China, I was a colonel in the occupying army in Manchuria. She comes from the Presbyterian tradition, I come from the Pentecostal. The world would think it impossible that she and I should love each other. But Christ has broken down all the barriers that should divide us. We are one in Christ Jesus."

If only all of us could hear that word. And I don't believe this oneness is for Christians alone. God loves the whole world. We all belong to one another whatever our belief or non-belief.

The influence of Japan is evident in my work. My first three novels are set there, as well as the beautiful picture book *The Tale of the Mandarin Ducks*, whose illustrations by Leo and Diane Dillon garnered a Boston Globe–Horn Book Award. I even had the chance to translate two Japanese folktales illustrated by the Hans Christian Andersen Medal–winning illustrator Suekichi Akaba, *The Crane Wife*, a *New York Times* Best Illustrated Book, and *The Tongue-Cut Sparrow*.

I've been back to Japan only twice since I left there, and my Japanese is so rusty I hardly dare open my mouth when I have a chance to speak it, but I couldn't be the writer I became without those four years spent there. To be loved by people you thought you hated is an experience I wish everyone could have.

Newly married John and me.

Another Countship

When our older son, John Jr., announced his engagement, his younger brother said to me, "I'm afraid John is rushing into marriage."

"David," I said, "rushing into marriage is not meeting someone one year, becoming engaged the next year, and marrying her the following year. Rushing into marriage is meeting someone in February, seeing him a few times in between, and marrying him in July." But since his father's and my marriage has worked out

189

just fine over the last fifty years, it's hard for me to argue against "rushing into marriage."

As I said earlier, I was all set to go to Yale Divinity School after my four years in Japan when a fellow missionary persuaded me to go to Union Seminary in New York City instead. I was a bit terrified at the thought of going from rural Japan to the metropolis of New York, but it turned out to be a life-changing year. I lived in an apartment on the campus with four other women students and we were a wonderfully congenial bunch. Four of us had been out of school doing other things before we came back for Union degrees, so at the advanced age of twenty-nine, I was grateful to be living with grown-ups and not fresh-faced college graduates.

At the orientation session all entering students were asked to take personality tests—to see if we were fit for the work for which we were preparing—and told that if we wanted to have a session with one of the deans about the results, we were welcome to make an appointment to do so. It seemed like a great opportunity to find out about all my hidden personality defects, so I immediately signed up for a session with the Dean of Women to go over my profile.

Dean Craig was one of the world's choice people. She was very reassuring about the state of my mental health, which she declared hardy, but there was one thing there that puzzled her. "The profile," she said, "indicates that you have some difficulty relating to men. I found this hard to believe, so I made a point in watching

College graduation day with Hazel.

you in the refectory, and I noticed you always head for a table where there are no male students. Don't you like men?"

"Yes, theoretically," I said, "but they don't seem to like me. My last three serious boyfriends all dumped me."

"Are you interested in being married?" she asked.

"Well, yes," I said, "but I love my work in Japan, and I'm not eager to be hurt again."

She gently suggested that for the last four years, I had been pretty isolated from Americans, especially eligible young men. I needed practice in just being comfortable around the opposite sex. Why didn't I begin by sitting at a table in the refectory where there were at least some men to talk with while I ate.

I made the mistake of sharing my session with Dean Craig with my apartment mates, who couldn't help teasing me about my "practice sessions" at mealtimes. I began to date at Union, and enjoyed myself, but they were all practice sessions. There wasn't anyone that I was really interested in as a prospective mate. I was all set to return to Japan as the stereotypical single lady missionary—like Katharine Hepburn in *The African Queen,* though not nearly as thin.

Then in February I got a phone call from a professor's wife. There were two young ministers at her door who were at the end of their two-week continuing education seminar and hoping for an evening of bridge before they headed back to their parishes. Her husband was out of town, so she was wondering if there were women in our apartment who'd like to play. I didn't play bridge, but Beverly and Meribeth did, and they were delighted for a chance to entertain the young ministers.

When the two men arrived, my friends were in their rooms primping a bit, and so I answered the door and stayed to chat until Beverly and Meribeth emerged and the bridge game could begin. I started to take my leave, when one of them asked if I'd like to stay and learn how to play. No, I said, I needed to study. At just about that time my major professor, who lived across the hall, knocked on the door and asked me if I was free to walk to the deli with him. He was extremely busy, and this was the only time he knew of that we could consult about my thesis. So I left the bridge party, had my thesis consultation, came back, said good night to all, and went to my room to work.

Early the next morning the phone rang. The caller identified himself as John Paterson, one of the two bridge-playing ministers. I presumed he'd called to speak to Beverly or Meribeth, but no, he wanted to speak to me. He wanted to ask me to have lunch with him. Well, as you know, I needed practice, so I said yes and met him at the appointed time in the refectory. We had lunch and, as I recall, a perfectly casual conversation, and when it was over, he asked me if I'd take a walk. He was a pleasant, good-looking young man, and I could always use more practice, so I said yes again.

Now, I can't relate the exact words. I think I went into a state of shock as this near stranger explained that he had to leave to go back to Buffalo that evening, but that—what on earth was it he said? Anyhow, I was sure from what he said that this young, very handsome young man that I had hardly met, had decided he wanted to marry me. Needless to say, I thought he had lost his mind.

I'm not sure what prompted me in my weekly letter home to mention quite casually that I had had lunch with a young Presbyterian minister from Buffalo. My mother rushed over to her best friend's house with the terrible news. "Katherine has gotten involved with a minister from Buffalo." "Well, that's wonderful," Helen said. "If Katherine marries him, she'll stay in this country and won't go back to Japan alone." "But I've *been* to Japan," my mother said. "I've never *been* to Buffalo." I was still considering John nuts. I mean, I was never the girl that all the boys fall for, but Mother, apparently, was already on John's wavelength.

Beginning as soon as John got back to Buffalo on Tuesday,

I was barraged by phone calls and letters from the handsome stranger. My apartment mates couldn't believe what had happened, and many wry comments about my successful practice sessions were thrown about. I was still convinced that this John Paterson (I soon learned there was only one *t* in his name) was out of his mind. He would call and I would answer the phone and hear this strange New England voice. Growing up in the South, to me the cultivated Southern voice has always been beautiful to the ear, and this Yankee speech seemed totally alien. If I *were* to marry him, I thought, all my children would talk like Yankees. It was impossible to contemplate. Besides, he was far too handsome. How could I trust any man that good-looking?

In addition to the letters and phone calls, there were the visits. Between the middle of February when we met and the end of March, John came to see me. He'd catch the midnight bus from Buffalo after his Sunday duties were done, spend Monday in New York courting me, and catch the midnight bus back so as to be on the job Tuesday morning. He was tired, and I was frantically trying to get my work done for school, so these visits were far from idyllic.

In March he suggested that I come to Buffalo to see him during my Easter break. I did not walk, I ran to see Dean Craig. "This crazy man wants me to come to see him in Buffalo!"

To my surprise, Dean Craig thought it was a good idea.

"But if I come he'll think I'm ready to marry him."

"I thought you said you'd like to get married."

194

"Well, yes, but I don't even know him."

"Well, how did you plan to get to know him?"

I explained that I was due to go back to Japan after graduation. We could write and stuff and then after I got to know him . . .

"Katherine," she said, "John is ready to get married. If you go back to Japan, you'll never see him again." I knew she was right. I couldn't get to know him unless I went, but that didn't mean I wasn't scared to death at the idea of spending a week on his turf.

So it was with Dean Craig's encouragement and my stomach in knots that I took the bus to Buffalo in April. We were married in July. Just a note about the actual proposal. When he asked me to marry him that Easter, John said that he knew I was a strong woman with many gifts, and he wanted to promise me that he would never stand in the way of my exercising those gifts. As I've said before, he didn't know when he said those words that he would be creating a Frankenstein monster, but despite the books and awards and notoriety, he's always been my chief supporter and has never stood in my way.

When we'd been married for enough years to be the parents of four lively children, we were living in Takoma Park, Maryland. Dean Craig had moved to Washington after her retirement, and we saw her a number of times before her too-early death. She confessed to me that in 1962, after she had urged me to go to Buffalo, she was seized with the fear that she might have done the wrong thing. All her training in counseling was of the indirect school. A counselor was never to prod a client on a particular course—simply help her to see the alternatives and let her make her own choice. She had never met John and she really knew nothing about him. So while I was in Buffalo, she went to the confidential files for 1953–56 and looked up John Barstow Paterson, and to her immense relief found nothing but raves.

In 1967 when we were applying to adopt our daughter Mary, the social worker did individual interviews with John and me. "Why did you marry your husband?" she asked. I was a bit taken aback and fumbled for an answer. It wouldn't be quite true that I had been madly in love—I hardly knew the fellow at the time. "Well," I said. "He asked me, and I liked him a lot."

It seemed a pretty puny answer regarding a person whom I now really and truly loved. I couldn't wait to hear John's answer. "What did you say when she asked you why you married me?" I asked. He replied, "I said I married you because I wanted to marry a grown-up, not somebody I'd have to raise." Whether I was worthy of this compliment might be debatable, but I still treasure it.

Soon after Lin came.

Motherhood

Many of the young girls I talk with these days want to grow up to be famous. I probably wanted to be famous too, sort of—I mean, why else would I so love performing that I dreamt of becoming a movie star? But even more than famous, I wanted to grow up to be a mother. Outdoors, with the boys on Piedmont Avenue, I played street football, marbles, and junior commandoes, but in my secret indoor life I cherished my dolls. They would have to do until I grew up and had real children. As it turned out, I had four children in just over four years, but for a long time it looked as though there'd be none at all.

Nearly all my friends and classmates had become parents while I was still a single lady missionary in Japan with no prospects of a husband, much less children. I remember standing on the train platform in Ashiya one day surrounded by small black-haired Japanese school children, saying wistfully to myself: "I want one of those." But back in the late fifties and early sixties, single women were not allowed to adopt children, so it looked, as I approached my thirties, as though I would miss out on my dream of motherhood.

But then, when I was twenty-nine I met John Paterson and we were married the summer before we both turned thirty. On our honeymoon we decided that we would have four children—two the old-fashioned way and two by adoption. We were both concerned that the world's population was exploding, and that in that population were children who needed families. The adopted child would come first. It would give him or her status as the eldest.

In Japan I had visited orphanages for the children born to Japanese women, children whose fathers were members of the American occupation. These children had no place in either country. We had been married less than a month when I wrote to a friend who did social work in Japan and asked her to make inquiries for us. My Japanese was still quite good in those days. It made perfect sense to us that we should adopt one of these forgotten children. My friend wrote back at once saying that it would not be possible. The Japanese government had just passed a law that Amerasian children in Japan could only be adopted into families in which at least one of the parents was Japanese. The fact that the orphanages were full, with almost no eligible parents stepping up to adopt, seemed to be beside the point. This law was later changed, but at the time it effectively ruled us out. However, my friend gave us the address of International Social Service, an agency that was doing adoptions of children from Hong Kong and Korea. My Mandarin was gone and I had never spoken Cantonese, but I did have roots in China, so we applied for a child from Hong Kong.

A social worker came out from a Buffalo agency and did a case study and then there was nothing to do but wait. We bought a child's rocking chair as a sort of talisman for the child we were waiting for, and I would look at the chair and daydream about a little girl with black hair sitting in the chair and rocking happily. But the wait went on. At this rate, we thought, we'd soon be too old to have those two homemade children. But a pregnancy that started out with hope ended in a miscarriage.

After the miscarriage, the prospect of motherhood seemed as dim as it had been since before my marriage. No progress was being made on the adoption front in the more than a year since our initial inquiry, and I didn't seem to be able to conceive again. We moved to Princeton so that John could pursue a graduate degree at Princeton Seminary and where, as I said earlier, I started teaching at the Pennington School for Boys. John had accepted a part-time job as assistant pastor in the First Presbyterian Church, and not long after we arrived in town, the senior pastor and his wife invited us for dinner. The door was opened by their pre-school son, who asked where our children were. I said we didn't have any children.

"Don't you want to have some children?" Wayne asked.

"Yes," I said, "but we just don't have any."

"Pray to Jesus," he said, as though that would solve everything. Don't ask me to explain it, maybe Wayne started praying for this poor childless couple; at any rate, in a little more than a month, John Jr., was on the way.

At almost the same time that I found out I was pregnant again, we got a call from one of our references in the Buffalo area to say that International Social Service was trying to locate us. Did we still want a child? Of course we did. The agency sent us a picture of the little girl they had matched with us. She was a determined-looking six-month-old with huge dark eyes and fierce black hair that stood straight up on her head. We fell in love at first sight. The orphanage had given her a name—Yeung Po Lin. The Po meant "precious" in the Canton dialect and was also part of my own Mandarin Chinese name, which was *Wong Ja Bao* or *Wong* (our family surname *ja*, a middle name we all had, and *bao*, "precious"), and her birthday was October 30—the day before my Halloween one. Surely she was meant to be our daughter.

But there was a problem. The state of New Jersey would not

recognize the family case study that had been done in Western New York. We would have to start all over again. New Jersey prided itself on very low taxes, which translated means very few government services, so by the time a social worker came to our apartment I was great with child. She took one look at my stomach and decided that John and I were out of our minds. Why would we be trying to adopt when we could obviously have children? She went off on her own maternity leave and never finished the home study, but fortunately another much more sympathetic worker was put on our case. The following June, John Jr. was born. Still nothing was happening with the adoption process and our daughter was spending her first two years in an overcrowded Hong Kong orphanage.

Our friendly social worker would not give up and kept pushing until she found out that our papers were languishing on some bureaucrat's desk because on some of the pages Paterson was spelled with one *t* and on others with two. Then, when everything seemed cleared up, there was a chickenpox epidemic in the orphanage and little Po Lin was not to be allowed to leave until all danger of contagion was past.

When we were sure that our daughter was truly coming, we began eagerly to tell family and friends what was about to happen. My China-loving parents were overjoyed—a Chinese granddaughter in the family—but John's father was deeply concerned. He predicted darkly that a child who had spent her first two years in an orphanage would never be able to trust or to adapt to family life. One of the friends we felt closest to in Princeton was appalled. How could we do this to little John? He would never recover from the shock of a sudden sister. And how dare we snatch a child from her own culture and bring her into our own? My confidence was shaken. We were taking a two-year-old out of the only life she knew and plunking her into an environment that would be alien in every way. I had no worries about happy little John Boy—I was sure he would quickly adapt—but what about our new child? What were we doing to her?

At just this time, I went to a weekend private school retreat with several of my students. One of the teachers that I met there was Chinese, so I screwed up my courage and asked him if I could speak with him privately. He listened thoughtfully as I told him what we were proposing to do and how some of our closest friends and family members were telling us that we were making a huge mistake. What did he think? Were we being fair to this child?

"I've just met you this weekend and I don't know your husband at all," he said. "But I know enough about the situation in Hong Kong that I can promise you that whatever you give this child will be better than what she has to look forward to there." His words somehow assured us that it would be all right to proceed as planned.

We began to think seriously of names for our new daughter. We wanted to keep her Chinese name, Po Lin, but we wanted her to have an English first name that would be special to our family. My grandmother was Elizabeth, my mother was Mary Elizabeth, and my older sister was Elizabeth, so we settled on Elizabeth PoLin Paterson and began trying out various nicknames. My older sister was Liz, an improvement on Lizzie, to be sure, but Liz seemed too old a nickname. I looked at the rocking chair and imagined a pig-tailed daughter called Betsy.

The long-awaited day finally arrived. Our daughter would be handed over to us planeside in LaGuardia Airport. The three of us waited—John was holding six-month-old John Boy and I was trying to hold myself together. John and I were excited and terrified. The baby, even far past his bedtime, was his usual bouncy happy self. There was another family waiting for their new daughter as well. In addition to the parents, there were three older children, thrilled with the thought of a new baby sister. We exchanged nervous conversation with the parents and took each other's addresses. Finally, after all the passengers had deplaned, a flight attendant appeared carrying a chubby smiling baby. The other family's name was called and, as the mother stepped forward to claim her, the little girl put out her arms. "Mama!" she said.

"*Your* baby is coming." The way the flight attendant was not smiling when she said it made me even more anxious. What was the matter with *our* baby?

At length a Chinese woman emerged. She looked exhausted, and the tiny, dazed little girl she handed to me simply flopped in my arms. "She hasn't slept since we left Hong King," the escort said, indicating that neither had she. I struggled to hold our new daughter. She weighed hardly anything but she was totally limp. *Had she never been cuddled?* I couldn't help but wonder what we had gotten ourselves into.

We drove back to Princeton that night, and my new daughter dozed off in my arms. We'd put a crib for her in John Boy's room, thinking that having another child about would feel less lonely than a room alone, but the moment I put her down in the crib she woke with a start and began to cry. That was Tuesday night. Wednesday, Thursday, Friday, and Saturday nights were the same story. John and I took shifts walking the floor carrying her, because it was only when we were actually walking that she would fall asleep. If we stopped walking or worse, sat down, she'd wake up; if we tried to put her in the crib, she'd sit bolt upright and begin to cry.

She never smiled, but when she was sitting in her high chair at the dining room table she at least seemed content. One morning at about five I put her in the high chair and began to feed her. She ate, not greedily, but steadily, through four or more bowls of cereal and at least three eggs. At ten o'clock I put her down. She needed to know that there would be more meals to come—that she could count on three each day.

It was quickly apparent that our little daughter looked nothing at all like a Betsy. I called my mother on the phone. "She's too tiny to be called 'Elizabeth,' and 'Betsy' and 'Beth' just don't fit." "Why not Lin?" asked Mother, who had yet to see even a photo of the child. It felt perfect, and she's been Lin ever since.

Little John loved racing around in a walker and Lin steered clear of our tiny reckless driver, but otherwise, if she were put down in one spot, she would seem almost rooted to it until picked up and moved somewhere else.

Since neither John nor I had had any sleep to speak of by Sunday morning, I suggested he go on to church with John Boy, who loved the nursery at church (well, he pretty much loved everything), and I would stay home with Lin. We had a set of colored blocks of different shapes that fit neatly into a square box. Trying to entertain her that morning, I dumped the blocks out on the floor and showed her how they fit back into the box. Then I dumped them out again. She studied them and began very carefully trying to fit them back into place. *Oh, dear,* I thought. *This is too much for her. She's a two-year-old that has hardly slept for a week.* So I helped her rearrange the blocks so they would fit. She gave me the same determined stare that looked out from her baby picture, watched me finish the job, and then she picked up the box and dumped all the blocks on the floor. The look she gave me made me know I was not to help, so I put my hands in my lap while she proceeded to fit each block into the box. *It's going to be all right,* I thought. *She's really smart.*

A bit later the two Johns returned from church. The senior pastor had asked him that morning how things were going with our new daughter and John had told him how we were getting practically no sleep—that Lin was sleeping only when we were walking the floor with her. Dr. Meisel offered to call a church member, a psychiatrist, who happened to be Chinese; maybe Dr. Wong would have some ideas that might help.

By the time we'd finished lunch Dr. Wong called. He asked if he and his wife could drop by, not for a professional visit, but just in friendship. I still remember the thoughtful way he put it, reassuring us that he didn't expect the poor preacher's family to come up with his professional fee.

I put John Jr. down for his nap, and Lin was watching me wash dishes when the Wongs arrived. (It seemed a happy coincidence that we had the same Chinese name.) I heard Dr. Wong suggest to John that he take him in to see the bedroom. Mrs. Wong, a tall, strikingly beautiful Chinese woman, came to the kitchen door. Lin looked up at her as though startled. Then Mrs. Wong squatted down to Lin's level and, in a very gentle voice, said something to her in Cantonese. Lin gave her a long stare and then walked over to me.

"You don't need to worry," Mrs. Wong said quietly. "See? She's already chosen you to be her mother." I knelt beside my little girl and put my arm around her. She didn't pull away.

In the bedroom, Dr. Wong and John were consulting. The doctor suggested that John take the railing off the crib and lower it as much as possible. "That railing is in the way of her getting to her high chair, the one place in the house where she feels safe. And she probably slept much closer to the ground in the orphanage. You can put a mattress beside the crib, so if she rolls out, she won't get hurt." John fetched a mattress off a twin bed in the guest room, and then the men came to the kitchen. Lin had fallen asleep against my shoulder.

"She's asleep," Dr. Wong said. "Why don't you put her in the crib?"

I started to protest, that she would only wake up screaming, but he was the doctor, so I obeyed. I laid her in the crib, and sure enough she sat right up, but this time she looked around, took in the new set up and, without a sound, lay back down. She was still asleep when the Wongs left. She didn't sleep more than an hour that afternoon, and she didn't sleep through every night for several weeks, but it was the beginning of a new, much better time for us all.

Besides food, which she could never get enough of, Lin loved two things: a tiny rubber dog and John Boy. She wouldn't talk to Big John or me in Cantonese or English, but we could hear her talking to her baby brother in the bedroom. "Say, 'ball,'" she'd order. And at six months, John said "ball." And, certainly partly thanks to Lin's coaching, he was talking in complex sentences before he was two. In the hall there was a full-length mirror and Lin would take the dog to the mirror and have a whispered conversation. I was never sure in what language, but she and the dog were obviously chatting with their mirrored selves.

Changing John Boy's diapers was always a hilarious affair. I would tickle his tummy and he would shriek with laughter. Lin would stand by looking at this scene with what seemed to me a disapproving stare. But one day when I was changing her diapers she took my hand and put it on her tummy, so I tickled her. My reward was her first smile.

We took the children to Winchester to meet my parents in February. We felt by then that Lin was comfortable enough in her new home to risk a trip away from it. As far as Lin and Mother were concerned, it was love at first sight.

By this time Lin was not only sleeping at night, she might

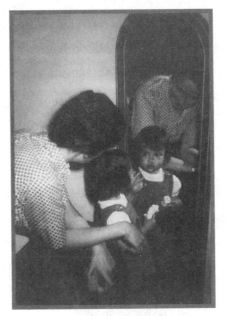

Lin talking to the mirror.

even take a nap. She was upstairs asleep when one of my mother's friends arrived carrying a Raggedy Ann doll she had made to give to our little new daughter. The friend was so proud of her handiwork, she wanted to rush upstairs and wake up Lin to give it to her. She was almost at the bottom stair before I stopped her.

The doll, like all Raggedy Anns, had bright orange wool hair, black button eyes, a red triangle of a nose, a sewn-on grin, but, unlike any I had ever seen, this doll was at least four feet tall. If your mother had read you stories about Raggedy Ann and Andy from the time you were a tot, you'd be thrilled to have a Raggedy Ann of your very own with a secret candy heart sewn inside. You might even like one more suitable to cuddling you than vice versa. But I was sure poor Lin would be terrified. I was afraid the sight of a stranger bearing a huge, even stranger doll would annul all the progress Lin had made.

As I was trying to suggest that we go cautiously, Lin appeared at the top of the stairs and looked down at us. The woman held out the doll.

"Baby!" Lin exclaimed, and came straight down the stairs to claim her new treasure, which was bigger than she was. Baby, she was never to know any other name, stayed with us until she was loved into literal rags.

And as for my unhappy father-in-law, before much time had passed, he'd forgotten all about his dire predictions. Lin had become his favorite of our children.

John Jr. was no longer John Boy when I realized the neighborhood children thought it was hilarious that I called my tiny son "Jumbo." It was the Southern accent that did it. I didn't want him going through life having people making fun of what his mother called him, so long before his second birthday he was simply "John," and, of course, the confusion of having two people by the same name in one family ensued. And, yes, I do remember his first complex English sentence, spoken when he was twenty-one months old. We were passing the public tennis courts in Silver Spring when he said: "When I get to be a big man, I play tennis ball like my daddy."

We moved to Maryland when David was well on the way, but we had to live for several months in an apartment in Silver Spring before the house we were buying in Takoma Park was vacated. So six days before David's actual birth, we moved into the house we would live in for the next thirteen years. The obstetrical practice recommended by my Princeton doctor worked out of George Washington University Hospital in downtown DC. I had nightmares of trying to get to the hospital through Washington rush hour traffic, but David conveniently decided to be born on Sunday morning. We went through nearly empty streets to the hospital, checked in, and David was born at eight a.m. It happened so quickly, the doctor almost didn't get there in time.

John welcomed his new son, and then went back and preached the Sunday sermon that he had written about the Prodigal Son. It was entitled "The Father's Two Sons." He thought that was a delightful coincidence. I only hoped that neither of our boys would turn out like the Biblical pair—the one a wastrel and the other a self-righteous prig.

Before long people began to remark how much our two boys looked alike and Lin began asking for a sister that looked like her. We had always planned to adopt a second child, but we now had three children and a mortgage and a very modest salary to support us all. The cost of adopting from overseas again would be beyond our means. We went to the local Lutheran Social Service that we were told was the best agency in the area and asked if they ever had an Asian or part Asian child available for adoption. They hadn't had such a child for years, they said, but they had just been asked to handle the adoption of American Indian children. Would we be interested? In the pictures the social worker showed us, there were many children who could pass Lin's test, so we agreed. Could we just wait, I asked, until David was at least two before we got a new baby? Even then we went from childless to the parents of four in four years and six weeks.

We were matched in the late spring of 1968 with a baby who was half Apache and half Kiowa. Her birthday was February 22, so her foster parents who had taken her home that day called her "Georgie" in honor of our first president. There was no way a daughter of mine was going through life with that name. So we spent a lot of time trying to figure out what to name her. We had thought we could wait to name her after we actually saw her, but a day before she was due to arrive, we were told that the state of Arizona was demanding a name to put on her amended birth certificate. We had decided on Mary, a family name on both sides, and the name of my closest friend from early days. We thought briefly of Mary Helen or even Helen Mary, which would combine my mother's name with that of my younger sister. John decided he preferred Mary Katherine, but Lin had kept her Chinese name. Wouldn't it mean something to Mary to have either an Apache or Kiowan middle name?

A member of our church in Takoma Park worked for the Bureau of Indian Affairs. I called Ken up and asked him if anyone in his office could help us. The problem was we had to send the name to Arizona by the end of the afternoon and it was already mid-morning.

About two hours later, we had a call from Ken. "Do you have pencil and paper handy?" he asked. When I did, he began to spell a name. It seemed to go on forever.

"Ken," I said weakly, "could we have something a little shorter?"

"Listen," he said sternly. "I called Will Rogers Jr. in Oklahoma and he sent a runner to the reservation to the old woman who gives names, and this is the name she sent back. I think you'd better keep it."

I showed the name to John. "Maybe we'd better drop the Katherine," I said.

He looked stricken. "But I've always wanted a little girl named Mary Katherine," he said. I doubted that, but we didn't have time to argue. We sent the name: Mary Katherine Nah-he-sah-pe-che-a Paterson. The name means: "Young Apache Lady." And we were right. She loved having that name. I asked Mary when she got married which of her many names she was going to drop, and she said, "None of them." So she is our five-name daughter, though she usually resorts to initials for the three middle names.

We went to the recently opened Dulles Airport to meet our new daughter. Two-year-old David and four-year-old John were racing back and forth across the giant, empty concourse that the airport was in those days. Lin was very still, and John Sr. and I were, as we had been when waiting for her, our nervous selves. At last the social worker came through the gate carrying a very large five-month-old.

"Can I hold her," asked tiny five-year-old Lin.

The baby was about as large as she was, but how could I say no? I told her to sit down and I would put her new sister on her lap.

Lin put her arms around Mary and gave a beatific smile. "She's got the same color hair, and the same color eyes, and the same color ears as me," she said.

Meeting Mary at the airport 1968. Social worker who brought her from Arizona on left.

Christmas 1970.

Motherhood
(Less than Ideal)

People who don't know me are prone to ask how I did it all—preacher's wife, four children, three dozen or so books, uncounted talks—how did I keep a proper balance? Balance? What balance? I feel as though I've teeter-tottered through the last fifty years, threatening to tip over at any time. I would never have made it without a supportive husband, forgiving children, understanding friends, and the grace of God. (And, as my grandmother used to say, "I speak reverently.") A few less than shining examples follow.

We had four small children and not much money, so buying new clothes was out of the question. I bought one new dress for Lin before she arrived. It was pale gray with beautiful smocking. Other than shoes and underwear I think that dress was the only brand-new item of that quality that I bought any of our children before the 1978 Newbery. What new clothes they had prior to that my mother insisted on buying. After the Newbery, royalty statement arrival day meant that each child could buy something brand-new for him- or herself that hadn't been previously worn by someone else.

From such humble sartorial beginnings, legends seem to arise. For example, my sons as young adults would insist to their friends that in elementary school we were too poor to buy them winter boots, so they wore plastic bread wrappers on snowy days. This is not true. There were bread bags involved, but they went on over street shoes, so that the winter boots that needed to last for more than one season could be slid on more easily. I promise you there were always boots covering the plastic bags, and if a boot had sprung a leak, the plastic helped keep the small foot dry.

This legend will never die because one summer day at our Lake George house my husband put plastic bags over his shoes and trousers so that he could protect them from flying grass while he wielded the weed-whacker. When one of our sons' college-aged friends happened to drive up to ask about the boys he caught John in this protective outfit. "You know," he later told the boys, "I never used to believe that story about the bread bags, but now . . ."

The faint line going up my sons' foreheads is another story. They will tell you that it is a Paterson genetic defect carried on the Y chromosome. "See," they'll say, "neither of our sisters has this line." The truth is much uglier. We had inherited from some now forgotten source a one-piece snowsuit that was fine in every respect but one. It had a very balky zipper and I had two very wiggly sons. Getting each leg into the proper legging pant was hard enough, but zipping from crotch to chin was nearly impossible. So it was that one horrible day I zipped eighteen-month-old John's forehead. I was devastated. My beautiful child would be scarred both physically and psychically for the rest of his life. We both got over the trauma, but exactly two years later—you guessed it—wrestling the same suit onto my second equally wiggly son, it happened again. As I said, I have forgiving children.

There were times, of course, when I had to forgive them—like the Christmas when David was an infant and Lin and John got up long before dawn and tore the wrappings off all the packages under the tree. I spent most of Christmas Day trying to put scraps of holiday paper together and figure out what scrap might have been around which relative's present. In the end I gave up and sent thank-you notes that read something like: Thank you for the (a) mittens (b) toy car (c) book (d) puzzle [choose one] that you gave to (1) Lin (2) John Jr. (3) David [check one].

Or there was the late afternoon when I thought the four of them were in the den watching Mr. Rogers on TV while I made supper, only to find that the older three had given their new baby sister war paint in varied colors with Magic Markers. I was appalled, but trying to follow the latest advice on child discipline, I didn't yell. I just said firmly: "Babies are not for coloring!" "Oh, yes," said four-year-old John, "I forgot. Jesus already colored her."

Actually, the three older children adored their new baby sister. The first Christmas after she came they asked for Indian costumes "so she'll feel at home."

I felt a bit stupid buying those cheesy outfits, but hardly anything they got in those years pleased them more. Mary was not, at the time, available for comment.

When, however, Mary could comment, she was very quotable. When she was three and the older children were all in school, her six cousins from Connecticut came for a visit. We were a popular visiting site for friends and relatives in those days, living, as we did, one block from the District of Columbia. The cousins took after their father. He was a dairy farmer, well over six feet and of Swedish ancestry, and all the cousins were tall young Swedes of boundless energy. The family wanted to spend one whole day exploring the zoo and kindly took Mary along.

When they returned rosy-cheeked and full of excitement, they brought with them a wilted little three-year-old.

"Are you tired, Mary?" I asked.

She raised her weary gaze to me. "My *socks* are tired," she said. "And my shoes won't even walk." To this day whenever in our family we want to express complete exhaustion, we employ Mary's eloquent description of her socks.

And speaking of shoes, there remains a mystery concerning them. Our very scrupulous pediatrician said that David should have orthopedic shoes to correct what she diagnosed as bow-leggedness. Trying to be at least as conscientious as the pediatrician, I took David (with, of course, three other children in tow) to the shoe store quite some distance away that sold such objects. The shoes were brown leather tie-ons, very ugly and very pricey. I swallowed and paid the bill so my little boy would not go through life afflicted, not dreaming that within a few weeks he would have managed to lose one of the hated shoes. Since he had no other shoes to wear to kindergarten, this meant another several hours taking four children to the distant shop to purchase another equally ugly and expensive pair, as the store was not in the business of selling single shoes. This scenario was repeated several times. Each time only one shoe was missing, but both shoes had to be replaced. The last time it happened was exactly one day after the new shoes had been purchased. When the five of us dragged ourselves into the store, the manager was amazed. "How in the world did you lose your shoe this time?" he asked David.

"I lost it dancing at a gerbil party," said David.

I didn't explain to the manager that Lin at nine was top sergeant of her little army of siblings whom she would order to perform various maneuvers. The gerbils needed entertaining, so Lin put a record on the phonograph and told the younger three to dance for the little caged creatures.

It was the end of buying special shoes for David, as just about that time I happened on an article that stated that most professional athletes were bow-legged. I had no such ambition for David but I figured bowed legs could not be a significant handicap. I did think when we cleared out the house on Albany Avenue to move to Norfolk, we would surely find the hidden trove of lost shoes, but we never did.

David was a preschool dropout, and I didn't even try to make him stick it out. The problem was his imaginary life, and I could never discourage another person's imaginary life, now could I? At three he would wake up every morning with a new persona. The one I remember best was "the forest ranger who stands in the tower watching out for forest fires." It was not sufficient to say "Good morning, Mr. Forest Ranger." If you wanted to greet him or get his attention, you had to say: "Oh, Mr. Forest-Ranger-who-stands-in-the-tower-watching-out-for-forest fires!" If you abbreviated it, or, heaven help us, addressed him simply as "David," you would get no response. This was complicated by the fact that the persona with the lengthy appellation attached changed daily. Mothers who are suckers for imaginative three-year-olds would play along, but harried nursery school teachers would send the offender to the time-out space. It seemed wiser to just skip the rest of preschool and let him play out all his fantasies with his adoring baby sister than to spend two years in time-out. I decided there would be plenty of years ahead when school attendance would be mandatory, why not delay what I accurately guessed might be a struggle to keep him in school?

The children's loving father was, to be honest, home for meals, but otherwise mostly keeping a pastor's long hours seven days a week. This didn't relieve him of anxiety about what was actually happening on the home front with his darling four while he was busy comforting the sick and dying elsewhere. He would walk into the house at suppertime, take one look, and ask what I had been doing all day. I would manage to declare weakly that I had kept his beloved children alive and well even if the house generally looked as though it had been invaded by a barbarian horde. Yes, I was trying to be a writer even back then, but I only wrote in those snatches of time when every child was safely in bed, or later, at school. Knowing my own powers of concentration, I knew that if I tried to write when I should be on duty as a parent, the house might well burn down while I was rearranging an awkward sentence. (Just one example: In a high school classroom my friend Barbara Thompson planned aloud a surprise party for me when I was sitting a few feet away reading. She knew I wouldn't hear a word. I didn't and was totally surprised.)

The summer after David was born was about the hottest summer I can ever remember. We had no air-conditioning, so I put Lin and John in bathing suits in the yard. The wading pool had an inch of water in it and I figured they could cool off a bit while I fed David. Within a few moments the phone was ringing. It was our next-door neighbor, a church member, as it happened.

"Katherine," she said in an obvious state of shock, "do you realize that your children are running around *naked* in the backyard?" My mental response, which, you'll be glad to know, I did not utter out loud was: *In this heat anybody with any sense would be running around naked.* I simply thanked her, sighed, put the baby down, and went out and wrestled the suits back on the children.

There was another morning that summer that I set up the two-sided easel in the yard with beautiful pots of primary colors and big brushes, figuring that art work would keep them busy while I gave poor David a little attention. I thought I was keeping an eye out the window, but the next thing I was aware of was an ungodly shriek and my husband's anguished cry of "Katherine!" I hurried out to see what disaster had occurred to find John holding his beloved children tightly. It seems that Lin and little John had had a wonderful time decorating not the newsprint on the easel, but each other with the crimson paint. As their father got out of the car, he saw his beloved toddlers racing toward him covered in blood.

When they got to school age, the children were often out playing in the small park a few steps up the street when he got home for supper. His invariable question when he walked into the house would be: "Where are the children?" And my invariable answer would be: "They're fine. They're up at the park playing. Children need some freedom. If I watched them every second we'd all be neurotic in no time."

It was many years later that I heard exactly what those boys were doing when I was assuring their father they were just fine. We had moved to Norfolk and I with two writer friends was going

When there were only two.

When there were only three.

My four.

back to Washington for a meeting. Teenaged David wanted to go along to visit some of his Takoma Park friends, and he was riding in the backseat with Stephanie Tolan. I abruptly aborted the front-seat conversation when I realized that David and Stephanie were talking about things they had done when they were young that they wouldn't want their mothers to know about.

It seemed that on more than one occasion when I was sure the boys and their neighborhood gang of friends were playing at the park just above our house, they were actually exploring the sewers beneath the city of Takoma Park. *Now* I can laugh. I can even imagine another answer to my husband's daily query about his children's whereabouts. "Down in the sewer, where else?"

They all survived the benign neglect of their mother. They slogged through years of public school and graduated from college. Eventually they married and presented us with matchless grandchildren. I did plenty wrong along the way, but they forgave me and survived to become delightful, imaginative human beings, and if my hair is almost white—well, it's the price of having been a less than ideal mother of four. In my defense, I did two things right. I loved them a lot, and even if I didn't spend nearly enough time cleaning the house they lived in, I made it up in countless hours of reading aloud.

Me and C.C.

Pets

Every pet the children had is a long story in itself, and we had almost every legal pet known to American life before we were through, but some of them were more memorable than others—notably Frank. On an excursion to DC's Rock Creek Park that neither parent was a part of, the boys came home with a native black snake—all black except for a tiny white chip on the right side of his lower lip. The argument they gave me was that Frank would be a companion to Sam, the baby boa currently in residence. In retrospect, Frank should have been named Francine, as there were unfertilized snake eggs to be found whenever Frank escaped his/her cage. And Frank made more escapes than Houdini. No matter how secure we tried to make the cage, Frank would find a way out, only to be found days later. Once, in the middle of the night, I met Frank coiled around the sink stand in the bathroom. Fortunately, I am not afraid of snakes.

I was at the time a part of a committee reluctantly appointed by the Montgomery Country Board of Education. Those of us in the poor east end of the county needed some of the perks that were being lavished upon the richer west side, and we were trying to come up with creative ideas to get our share. That particular evening the meeting was held in our living room and all of us were seriously struggling with an approach to parity for our children, when I spied Frank, who had been missing more than a week. Behind the glass front of the old secretary, I could see dark black loops.

"There's Frank!" I cried, startling my fellow committee members. "He's in the desk." The boys heard me and came running. But yanking an unwilling snake who has managed to wind himself in and out of the cubby holes of an antique desk is no simple matter. I think the committee gave up before we did and quietly adjourned themselves behind my back.

After the beloved Sam died, I suggested that Frank wasn't really happy in our home. He had no reptile companion, live mice were pricey, and besides, if he were content, why was he always escaping the cage to roam the house?

Reluctantly, the boys agreed. We made a real ceremony of it. All six of us went to Rock Creek Park to return Frank to the wilds from which he had come.

Some months later, David came racing into the house after school. "Guess who I saw today?" he cried.

"Who?"

"Frank!" he said. Their class had gone on a school field trip to the nature center in Rock Creek Park and there, in an enormous cage, was a "Native Black Snake" looking very sleek and basking in all the attention.

"How do you know it was Frank?" I asked. Coincidences on this order only appeared in Dickens.

"It was Frank all right. He had that little white chip right there on his lip."

The dogs were always my favorite pets, but we did have one very memorable cat, Charlie Chaplin, for his little black mustache, but always known as C.C. At the time that C.C. came into our lives we had Blossom, the springer spaniel, as well as other assorted creatures.

One late Friday afternoon when their father was away on a short study leave, John came home carrying a pasteboard box. On the outside of the box, in black marker, were the words "Free to a good home," and inside the box was the tiniest, most pitiful-looking kitten I had ever seen.

"Can we keep him?" John asked.

"No," I said firmly. "If your father comes home and finds I have let you all have yet another animal, he'll think I've lost my mind."

"But he was just on the picnic table at the park. If I take him back, the dogs will get him."

He had me there. There were a lot of neighborhood dogs who had never known a leash and who would undoubtedly be in the park that night. It was late Friday afternoon. The SPCA would have closed for the weekend. Besides, I was being picked up in a few minutes by friends to have a rare dinner out. There was no way I could deal with the pitiful little creature that evening. So I sighed and told John to get the poor thing some milk. I would deal with it in the morning.

Morning came and it was obvious to me that the kitten was on its last legs. I called the vet to see if they were open on Saturdays. They were, so I took the kitten over. Whatever the SPCA would do with it, I didn't want it dying on my watch.

I explained all this to the receptionist—that I was only trying to keep the thing alive until the humane society opened on Monday. Many dollars later I left the vet's, only to return that very afternoon, sure that this time the kitten really was dying.

When I paid another, for me, enormous bill, the receptionist was not even trying not to laugh. "Now, are you going to keep that kitten, Mrs. Paterson?"

I assured her I was not, but, of course, by Monday, we had all fallen in love with the piteous little creature who was almost too weak to meow. By the time John Sr. got home, and, as predicted, thought his wife had lost her mind, he had five of us pleading for C.C.'s life. Ironically, or perhaps because C.C. was a very clever cat, it was John Sr.'s lap he chose to sit on and purr. John softened, and many years later he said to me, "You know, if we were ever to divorce, I get the cat."

There is a postscript to this story. Long after C.C. had lived a happy life with us and departed peacefully, young John, now out of college and working in New York City took a course in creative writing at the New School. I was curious to know about the course and he told me the first assignment was to write a story from one's childhood. "So I wrote that story about how we got C.C."

There was something about the way he said it that made me inquire further.

"Oh, you know, the neighbors down the street had all these kittens they were giving away, but I knew that if I brought one home and told you where it came from you'd march me right back to return it, so . . ."

I was incredulous. "So you made up that whole thing about the box in the park?"

"Yeah, I told you that. I got a box and wrote 'Free to a good home' on it. I told you that years ago."

"You did not." Apparently, it was another of those things you did as a child you wouldn't want your mother to know about.

I was fond of C.C., but it has always been the dogs that I have loved most.

First there was Manch. He was my consolation after the miscarriage. He was half dachshund and half Manchester terrier. That may sound awful, but actually with the longish legs of a Manchester and the sweet face of a dachshund, he was a very handsome little fellow. And fellow he was. We hadn't realized that we should have had him neutered, and so he became the Don Juan of the canine world. Bolting out of the house whenever the door was cracked open, he sometimes was gone for more than a day. He often came home from these jaunts in wretched shape but he would heal to head out another day. Coming into my life when he did, he was utterly spoiled. A young German pastor, who lived with us while working for the summer with John, couldn't believe how spoiled Manch was—I treated him as though he were human. Win was flabbergasted when he heard me say to the dog: "We don't put our paws on the table while folks are eating, Manch."

"No wonder he thinks he's human with that name!" Winfred said.

"What?"

"Mensch!" he said. "It's the word for 'man.'"

But, then, to Manch's distress, we began to have children at a rapid rate. With each child he grew more jealous of all the attention being lavished elsewhere that used to be his alone. Finally, when David was a toddler, he decided that if you can't beat them, join them. As soon as David could reach the knob, Manch taught him how to open the door, and one day that door got opened and we never saw Manch again.

For years, while I was out driving, I would think I saw him and slam on the brakes to make sure. But it never was.

Manch is memorialized in a book I started when John Jr. was an infant. Standing at the window one snowy day, I watched Manch bounding through a foot of snowfall and thought: *I wonder where he's going in all that snow.* I wrote a couple of chapters, but I didn't know how to write a book and before long Lin arrived and I really forgot about my attempt to write about Manch. Many years later Avi asked me to contribute a serialized story for the newspapers in his Breakfast Serials project. Writing a newspaper serial is unlike any other kind of writing. Each chapter has to be three to three and a half double-spaced pages with the final page ending in a cliff hanger so patrons can hardly wait to buy the newspaper the following week to see what happens. You move from that opening to another cliff hanger at the end of that chapter and so on for twelve to fifteen chapters.

Aha! I thought. *That's how I can write Manch's story.* I dug my abandoned few chapters out of my messy files and they became *The Field of the Dogs* in the newspaper serial. Sally Daugherty, who edited the story for Breakfast Serials, then brought it out in book form at HarperCollins. The book opens with the words: *I wonder where he's going in all that snow.* The setting is no longer

New Jersey, it is Vermont, and the problems of the boy are different, but the hero dog is Manch as I remembered him.

Blossom was a gift from my parents. My mother had never liked Manch, probably because of his promiscuous ways, so she could hardly wait until he had disappeared to announce that they were going to give us a proper dog—a thoroughbred English springer spaniel. They had close friends who bred springers and we were to have one. I thought I needed a bit more time—what if Manch were to miraculously return?—and even not, I needed to mourn for him. What was all the rush? But our designated puppy was ready to be brought home right at Apple Blossom Festival time in Winchester, so the six of us went to get her. She was adorable, a tiny liver-and-white bundle who waddled on her short legs. We all fell in love at first sight. On her American Kennel Club registration she has a more dignified name, but we lost those papers years ago. The only name she ever knew was "Blossom."

Looking back, it's hard to remember Blossom ever doing anything wrong—well, that is, except when she ate the lightbulb, and she was hardly more than a puppy at the time.

I went into the den one night to find on the floor a chewed cardboard wrapper for a lightbulb, but when I looked for the bulb there was none—not even any glass—just a metal screw end. I was alarmed. My beautiful Blossom had eaten the bulb. I had read that if a child or an animal ate glass, you should feed them bread to keep the shards from cutting their innards. Fortunately, we had just been to the day-old bread store and had several two-pound loaves on hand. I fed Blossom an entire loaf, and was halfway through the second loaf when she let me know she'd had more than enough.

She seemed all right when I went to bed, and the next morning I was busy getting everyone off to school. It wasn't until after my husband had left for the office that I realized I hadn't seen Blossom all morning. I called and looked and finally located her in the dining room, tucked between the hutch and the wall corner. She looked at me sadly but didn't emerge. I tried to tempt her out with a piece of bologna. She didn't move. I put a hot dog just out of reach, thinking she'd surely come out and get it. She stretched her nose in that direction, but she only whimpered.

I had no car at the time, so I called John. "You've got to come home and take Blossom to the vet," I said. "She won't even come out to get meat."

John pulled Blossom out and carried her to the car and then into the vet's waiting room. She simply lay across his lap in a semi-comatose fashion. A woman came in carrying a sick cat. At this point in Blossom's life, she hadn't had a close personal relationship with a cat, and she was visibly alarmed. She began to shake so much that John, fearing she would fall, put her gently on the floor. She squatted and laid an enormous pile right on the pristine floor of the waiting room. Whereupon she stood up, tail wagging, completely cured.

The receptionist scurried to get cleaning equipment, and the vet appeared to see what all the commotion was about. John explained about the lightbulb, the bread, and her deadly appearance until this moment. The vet began to laugh. "Poor thing. She was so constipated from all that bread your wife gave her that she couldn't move."

Blossom grew more regal by the year, and then along came Princess, the least regal dog we ever owned. We had moved to Norfolk, taking only Blossom and C.C. with us, but, somehow, David was dissatisfied. He was very homesick for Takoma Park and, feeling friendless, brought home a little wild duckling from the bank of the nearby river. This was a very bad idea. The duckling agreed and immediately died to prove it.

"If you have to have another pet," I said, "you may have a puppy. We will go to the humane society and you may have the smallest dog there that isn't a Chihuahua."

We went, as I recall, the very next afternoon. In the stories, a puppy leaps out and licks the face of her rescuer, showing that it truly belongs. The puppy David chose hung to the back wall of the cage and didn't move. David reached in and pulled her out. Her pitiful state was, if anything, worse than C.C.'s the night he arrived.

"Are you sure?"

He was sure. He named her Princess. I never asked, but I suspected in honor of Prince Terrien in *Bridge to Terabithia*. My sister Helen's family came for a visit that first week. When I warned her in advance that we had a new puppy, she was appalled. She says that her first reaction was that I was crazy to let the children have another pet, but when she saw Princess, she thought: *Oh, well, it'll be dead in a week.*

But Princess thrived. She and C.C., who was larger than she was for quite some time, roughhoused like fond siblings. Occasionally, Blossom would go over and put her nose between them as if to say, *That's enough, children. You keep at it, someone's going to get hurt.* When Princess was rebuked or unhappy she would stick her back paw in her mouth and suck it exactly as a child will suck his thumb. It was a habit she never broke and she lived to be fifteen years old. If I don't confess it, my friends will wonder why not, but the fact is, once the children left home, Princess loved very few people. We warned every visitor not to pet her, but we have many friends who love dogs and were sure Princess could not resist them. They'd never met a dog who could. "See? She likes me," they would say, stroking her lovingly. At just about that moment Princess would snarl, and occasionally nip the startled visitor. It was very embarrassing, as dogs, they say, take after their owners. But we couldn't just get rid of her. She wasn't Frank that we could return to the wild. So we loved her and were loved in return by her until she died peacefully and is buried in our backyard.

We decided not to get another dog. It was a rational decision. We were traveling too much and getting to the point that yet another round of house-breaking was daunting. We missed having a dog, but we were not going to get another Princess who threatened all our friends with a growl or a nip. John's first cousin's wife raised golden retrievers—a perfect dog for people with lots of friends and small grandchildren. We didn't realize that several members of the family would find their allergies going haywire whenever they were around her. But aside from the family allergies and our never having a hairless garment, Annie was the perfect pet, the most beautiful, loving creature anyone could hope to know. She was, however, not without problems. If she gave others allergic reactions, she herself was plagued with allergies. We went through all the allergy tests, gave her the long series of allergy shots, spent more money at the vet's taking care of her ear and skin problems than I spent at the pediatrician's for all four children combined.

When she was nine, her lymph nodes swelled rather alarmingly, but we thought it was in reaction to her many ear infections. Then the vet suggested gravely that the nodes should be biopsied, in case it was more serious. He suspected lymphoma, but he couldn't be sure without the pathology report. Sick with dread, we agreed, and to our great relief the tests came out negative. The vet, who also loved her, was happy, but puzzled. He had been so sure. We lived in a fool's paradise for the next several months. When summer came and she seemed to be lethargic and panted excessively, we put it down to the unusually hot weather.

But one morning at Lake George I let her out. She always came right back, but that day she didn't. "She's gone to the woods to die," John said. And she had. When I found her hours later, she was still alive but she had made herself a little nest between

235

two logs. She looked up when she saw me coming with her usual sweet expression, but she did not move. I got three young men who were working nearby to help me get her into the car and we took her to the vet in Ticonderoga. When we got back to the house there was a message to call the animal hospital. She was in terrible distress and there was nothing they could do for her.

We went back to the hospital and were led into a small room. Two young women brought Annie in on a stretcher. She looked almost dead, but when we spoke to her, she sat straight up, wagged her tail and smiled her wonderful smile. After we both hugged and kissed her, she lay back down on the stretcher, her head on her paws, her eyes closed, and didn't move again.

We were devastated, but so was everyone who knew her. I had never seen an animal so beloved. We got the kind of messages that you get when a family member has died, everyone saying what a wonderful dog she was and how much they would miss her. "It's a bit sad when you remember that when poor little Princess died you and I were the only people in the world who mourned her," I said to John. Every card, letter, email, and call about Annie made us cry, but they were a real comfort.

Lin and her family came to Lake George not long after Annie's death, and Lin and our granddaughter Jordan decided that John and I needed a dog badly. They went on a website called Petfinder that lists dogs needing adoption in every part of the country. At one point they found the perfect dog for us in Florida. But I thought surely Vermont would have dogs needing rescuing, and indeed they do. So our lives have been made rich again with two-year-old Pixie (named after *The Flint Heart*). We're guessing she's a Maltese Yorkie mix—eleven pounds as opposed to Annie's nearly ninety—non-shedding and very much a lap cuddler. She had been found on the streets of Gainesville, Georgia, never claimed, and would have been euthanized except that a rescue transport team brought her to Good Karma Rescue in East Montpelier, Vermont, who certified us as a genuinely okay adoptive home.

John and Pixie.

The Newbery, 1981.

Motherhood As Inspiration

A man I had just met asked me what I did. When I replied I was a writer he said: "Oh, I know all about that. When I was a kid, my best friend's father was a writer. If we went to his house we had to tiptoe around. We couldn't make any noise at all because his dad was always working."

"You did say 'father,' didn't you?"

Because it's quite different, or at least it was in my day, if the mother is the writer. Four children take a lot of time, but I have said more than once that the people who took my time were the very people who gave me something worth writing about.

It began with the first novel. I started writing a novel, as I said, because nothing else I'd written was selling, and I thought I might be able to write a chapter a week and at the end of the year have a book. I wanted to write a story set in Japan, because I was a little bit homesick, both for Japan and that feeling of competency I had once had, back in the days when I was a confident young single woman. Besides, if I wrote a story set in the past, I would have an excuse to read Japanese history, something I loved doing. I don't think I even knew that if I did that I would be committing historical fiction. I wasn't thinking about genre, I was thinking about story. I'm sure I didn't realize that a book for young people set in twelfth-century Japan would be, for all practical purposes, totally unmarketable.

But a novel has to have more than a fascinating setting and well-paced plot. It has to have an emotional core. It has to be written out of passion. And the heart of this novel, set in twelfth-century Japan, came from an unexpected source. It came from six-year-old Lin.

As I indicated earlier, Lin's initial adjustment was difficult, and again when we moved from New Jersey to Maryland in 1966, a lot of it came unglued and had to be redone. But, by 1968, when she was five, then six, life had settled down pretty well for her. Still, there were times when for no reason we could discern, the bright, happy little daughter she had become would disappear.

In her place would be a silent waif. It was as though the child we knew had simply pulled down a curtain that we could not reach through.

This might go on for several days at a time, and it scared me to death. Where had she gone? What was she experiencing behind that blank stare? And how on earth could I reach her?

The curtain had been down for several days. I had tried everything—cajoling, begging, holding her. Nothing got through. One evening I was in the kitchen making supper when she came in. Without a word she climbed up on a high kitchen stool and sat there, her tiny body present, but the rest of her completely closed away. I tried to chat with her in a normal tone of voice. There was no answer, no indication that she even heard. The harder I tried, the more tense I became.

Finally, I did what any good mother would do under the circumstances. I lost my temper. "Lin," I yelled, "how can I help you if you won't tell me what's the matter?"

She jerked to life, her eyes wide open. "Why did that woman give me away?"

Then it all began to pour out. Why had she been given away? We'd never told her she was a foundling. It seemed too harsh– just that her mother had not been able to keep her and wanted her to have a home. I repeated this, adding that I was sure her mother hadn't wanted to give her away and wouldn't have if there had been any possibility that she could take care of her. Was her mother alive? Was she all right? I couldn't answer her questions, but she let me try to comfort and assure her. She never again, even in adolescence, pulled down the curtain in just that way.

She is a mother now herself—a wonderful, loving, funny mother. I watched her giving her own babies all the care that she herself never had as an infant, but that somehow she knew how to give. She is a wonder and I cannot tell you how much I admire her.

But in the context of this story what she gave me that day was not only herself, but the emotional heart of the novel I wanted to write. What must it be like, I wondered, to have a parent somewhere whom you do not know?

I look at *The Sign of the Chrysanthemum* and it's no marvel to me now that I had difficulty finding a publisher. It is set in the midst of the civil strife of twelfth-century Japan. The central character is a thieving bastard who is searching for the father he never knew. The girl he cares about ends up in a brothel. I didn't put her there because I wanted to scandalize my readers, but because a beautiful thirteen-year-old girl in twelfth-century Japan who had no one to protect her would, most likely, end up in a brothel, and the penniless teenaged boy who loved her would be powerless to save her.

Now, at some point I must have realized that I hadn't seen a lot of books for young readers along this line, but when I wrote *The Sign of the Chrysanthemum* I wasn't, to be honest, worrying about readers. I was writing a story I needed and wanted to write, as honestly and as well as I knew how.

For any of you out there who have wondered about the dif-

241

First draft
of first chapter —

Numa ~~sat~~ sat on the dirt floor with his eyes downcast, while his face *a* perfect mask of mourning ~~While~~ the Sato's toothless ~~old~~ wife ~~washed~~ bathed the wasted corpse that had been his mother.

a kimono?
"Did she have a kimono for her burial?"

The boy got up, then, wordlessly + fetched ~~to~~ from the ~~tiny~~ chest the one decent garment his mother had ever owned. She had never worn it, ~~saving~~ ~~for it,~~ ~~in her pathetic way, for the one occasion~~ ~~of her life which promised a little dignity.~~ It had been saved for this day.

She would not want me to weep for her, he told himself. Her life was only grief + death is her release. And mine — his heart beat faster. And mine — For now — nothing held him ~~as soon as he had~~ ~~crossed the~~ Yashima — he could make his way to the capital + begin his search.

~~Take word of the peasant Sato~~
~~Sato thrust his~~

An ugly peasant face was thrust into the doorway — "The priest has come," ~~The peasant face was~~ Sato's voice was drawn out in a solemn manner so unsuited to his comical features that Numa laughed ~~behind his mourning~~ inside his belly.

First draft of *The Sign of the Chrysanthemum*.

ference between novels for the young and adult novels, the adult best seller at about the same time my book was published—a best seller that, by the way, was breaking every sales record since *Gone with the Wind*, was the sentimental, moralistic tale of an over-achieving seagull.

Then how on earth did my book ever see the light of day? Granted, it almost didn't. It made the rounds of various publishers for more than two years. And then a miracle happened. It was taken out of the seventh or eighth publisher's slush pile by a young Sandra Jordan, who read it and loved it. She took it to her boss, the senior editor, who had recently returned from a visit to Japan and who was and is a woman of vision in the field of children's books. She has always dared to publish books that she felt would open up unknown worlds for children. I'm sure Ann Beneduce had no illusions that the book would sell well. She hoped, of course, that it would sell respectably, but she wanted young readers to have a chance at the book, and she wanted the writer of it to have the chance to write more books.

In 1970 Ann Beneduce handed my manuscript to an editor who was just coming off maternity leave. I can promise you, if that had not happened, I would not be writing this book, for that first editor, Virginia Buckley, has been the editor of all my novels. And if my books are good, it is because Virginia would never let me stop working until they were.

But outwardly he was the grief stricken orphan as he rose quietly & usher the priest into the hut.

~~There~~ had so little food to offer the few peasants who had come to mourn that by ~~midnight~~ nightfall the last one had shuffled home leaving him alone to ~~light the candles and pray~~ light the taper and pray.

The ~~two~~ candles pricked two holes in the darkness. For the first time the tiny hut seemed large with loneliness. Muna did not ~~try to~~ ~~pray~~ ~~kneel~~ sat ~~cross legged~~ before ~~them~~ the makeshift altar hugging his knees. She was gone, after all. ~~The only one~~ who cared for him until now. ~~They had been~~ like ~~the~~ two candles in a dark & unfriendly world. Tears came into his eyes. ~~So little~~

Even as a child he had pitied his mother.

"He was very ~~tall~~ big, your father," he remembered her voice like a little girls breathless. "A fine Samurai. Oh such beautiful armour. And such a sword — taller than you are now."

Mary helps edit.

Of Nightingales That Weep, my second novel, also set in twelfth-century Japan, was written before the first was published. I was already to write another, but, alas, I had no ideas for a new book. I had four children, though, why not ask them?

There was no debate. They all wanted a mystery story. I really like a good mystery story, but I am realistic enough to know that they aren't easy to write. It seemed to me that it took the same kind of brain that it took to win at chess, and Lin had been beating me at chess for the last five years. "Do you think," I asked my eager children, "that anyone who is regularly beaten at chess by a six-year-old has the kind of brain it takes to plot a mystery story?"

At just about that time, I saw in *The Washington Post* an advertisement for Bunraku, the Japanese puppet theater. The Osaka Bunraku Company was coming to perform at the Kennedy Center. My mind went back to puppet performances I had seen during my days in Japan. The main theater had been destroyed during the war, so the theater I went to was small and dark. Patrons took their lunches for the several-hour play and sat on tatami mats to watch. As humble as the surroundings might have been, the puppets and scenery were magnificent. The puppets in Bunraku are nearly life-sized and manipulated by three people—one does the feet, another the left hand and the master puppeteer does the head and right hand. In most scenes all the puppeteers are under black hoods except the master, who is dressed in formal kimono. You would think that the audience would be fascinated by the puppeteers, but even the unhooded master is soon forgotten as the puppets themselves seem to come to life before your eyes. There is something a bit spooky about the puppets, so lifelike, but not really alive. What a marvelous setting for a mystery, I thought, but then remembered that I really was not up to writing one. So the children and I compromised. I would try to write an adventure story with as much suspense as possible.

As I was reading everything I could get my hands on about Bunraku, I had what some people call a waking dream. In it I saw a boy in the upper story of an old Japanese warehouse. The place was filled with trunks, and costumes hung from the ceiling. The only light came from a single window at the far end of the room. The boy was scrabbling about looking for something—something that he could not find. Then I heard heavy footsteps coming up the staircase, and in the dim light I saw the white face of a warrior puppet. Behind the puppet, a hooded figure was manipulating the head and right hand of the puppet. And in the hand was a samurai sword.

That was all I got—the boy vainly looking for something and a menacing hooded figure manipulating a sword-wielding puppet. So I had to write *The Master Puppeteer* to find out who the boy was and what he was looking for and who was trying to frighten him and why.

I knew I couldn't write about Bunraku without going back to Japan and seeing more plays and interviewing puppeteers and historians of the puppet theater. I had four young children and very little money, so that seemed impossible. But my husband suggested

I ask for a larger advance on *Of Nightingales That Weep*, which I did with fear and trembling, but the publishers doubled my advance from one thousand to two thousand dollars. This allowed me, not only to go to Japan, but to take ten-year-old Lin with me. From Japan we went on to Hong Kong so that she could visit the orphanage where she spent her first two years, something she had often said she wanted to do.

When we got back from that wonderful trip, I was very tired. I tried to get back to writing the book, but everything I wrote seemed dry and lifeless. The extreme tiredness proved to be a symptom of cancer. After my hospital stay I began to write again, but I had lost any confidence in my ability to write the book. I decided to read it aloud one stormy night in the barn we rented at Lake George. The electricity was off and candlelight seemed appropriate to the story. The next day I caught John Jr. rifling the drawer to read ahead. I was thrilled. The story was working. And so *The Master Puppeteer* was born. When the Mystery Writers of America gave me a special award for my non-mystery book, I was almost as proud of the citation as I was of the National Book Award that the book also garnered.

If the fourth grade at Wiley School was the most miserable year of my childhood, I think I would have to choose 1974 as the most painful year of my adult life. I was working on *The Master Puppeteer* when I was sent to the hospital to see about a suspicious lump that turned out to be a malignancy. It is obvious that I survived my bout with cancer. In the years since I have enjoyed remarkably good health, but in 1974 I didn't know what the future would be or if I had one to look forward to. Now, children are often afraid of death, and I certainly was as a child. But I was

The puppeteer in the center was my chief resource in writing The Master Puppeteer.

forty-one years old now with four young children, and it was not only the dread of dying, but the idea of leaving my children behind that I could not bear to imagine. I knew my lovely husband would be fine. There would be women lining up around the block to snatch him the moment I was out of the picture. One of them might even turn out to be a better mother than I was. But, surely, no one, I thought, no one, however fit to replace me, could ever love those children the way I did.

Of course, my death would not leave my children alone. They had a loving father and grandparents and aunts and uncles and a whole congregation of people who would care for them. Lin and John were not only brother and sister, but the closest of friends. Mary had a wonderful teacher, with a daughter just Mary's age who looked out for her while I was in the hospital and, would, I knew, continue to care for her. And David had Lisa.

Lisa had come into our lives the previous autumn. The small school that our children attended was closed and all the students were moved to a much larger elementary school across town. David, our second grader, was miserable. In the little school he was both the class artist and the class clown. In his new school he was simply weird. Every day he came home and declared that he was "never, never going back to school and you can't make me." And I, his mother, who had been in fifteen different schools by the time I was eighteen and had been initially despised at nearly every one, was over-identifying with my seven-year-old, probably exacerbating his misery, but, nevertheless getting him up every morning and grimly pushing him out the door, fearing that his unhappiness would never end.

Then one afternoon, our bright funny little boy that I thought was gone forever came running into the house. "Me and Lisa Hill are making a diorama of *Little House in the Big Woods*," he announced cheerily. I had never heard the name before, but from then on I was to hear hardly any other name. "Now, I'd like to promise you girls," I say when I'm talking to children, "that I was thrilled that my son's best friend was a girl. But unfortunately, all I could think was 'They thought he was weird before. If his best friend is a girl, he'll never fit in.'"

But then I met Lisa, and my worries evaporated. Anyone would be fortunate to have her for a best friend. She was bright, imaginative, and funny. She laughed at his jokes and he at hers. She was the only girl daring enough to invade the second-grade boys' T-ball team. She and David played together after school in the woods below her house and talked to each other in the evenings on the phone.

"It's your *girlfriend*, David," his older brother would say.

But David would take the phone unperturbed. Girlfriends are people who chase you down on the playground to grab you and kiss you. Lisa was no more a "girlfriend" than Margaret Thatcher was a Playboy Bunny.

Then on an August morning, the phone rang. It was a call from the Hills' next-door neighbor. "I thought you ought to know," Mrs. Robinson said, "that Lisa was killed this morning." While the family was on vacation at Bethany Beach, on a day when the lifeguards sensed no danger from thunder far off in the distance, a joyful little girl, dancing on a rock above the crowded beach, was felled by a bolt of lightning from the sky.

How was I to make sense of this tragedy for my child? I couldn't make sense of it for myself. So, eventually, I began to write a story, because I knew that a story has to make sense. It has a beginning, a middle, and an end, and when you get to the end, even if you cannot articulate intellectually what has happened, you know emotionally that you have come from chaos to order. In *Thus Spoke Zarathustra,* Nietzsche says: "One must have chaos within to give birth to a dancing star." And somehow, as dark as life itself sometimes seems, at the end of a well-told story, the dancing star will shed light on the chaos.

So I began to write what I could not understand or explain, but when I came to the place in my story when I knew that if I went to work the next day I would write the chapter in which Leslie Burke would die, I did the only thing I could do to keep her alive, I didn't go to work. I caught up on my mail, I rearranged my bookshelves, I think I was even reduced to scrubbing the kitchen floor—anything to keep from writing the fatal chapter.

It was just then that I happened to have lunch with a former Richmond classmate. "How's your new book coming?" she asked. Now, no one, as the long-suffering members of my immediate family know all too well, no one is ever supposed to ask me how my work is coming, but Estelle had known me longer than any of them, and she had no respect. So I blurted out an answer. "I'm trying to write a book about a friendship between a boy and a girl in which the girl dies," I said. "But I can't let her die. I guess," I added, thinking I was very wise, "I guess I can't face going through Lisa's death again."

Estelle looked me straight in the eye. "I don't think it's Lisa's death you can't face," she said. "I think it's yours."

I knew she was right. If it were Lisa's death I couldn't face, it was one thing, but if it were my death I couldn't face, then I would have to finish the book. I went home that afternoon, and with sweat pouring down my arms, wrote the chapter and in a few days finished the draft. It was the most painful writing I had ever done—so painful I simply couldn't stand having it in the house, so I did what no real writer would ever do, I mailed the draft to Virginia Buckley before the sweat had evaporated.

As soon as I mailed the manuscript, I knew that I had made a terrible mistake. Every day I expected the letter that would tell me politely, maybe even a little sorrowfully, that I had obviously lost whatever talent I had shown up until then—that my career as a writer was over. Instead I got a phone call. It was Virginia, saying that she wanted to talk to me about my new manuscript. I stopped breathing.

"I laughed through the first two-thirds," she said, "and cried through the last." I began to breathe again. "Now," she continued, "let's turn it into a book."

And then she did what I believe the great editors do; she asked me the question that would do just that. "Is this," she asked, "a story about friendship or is it a story about death?"

Until that moment, I had thought I was writing a story about death. Hadn't it been a year of death in our lives? But as soon as she asked the question, I knew I was wrong. "Oh," I said, "it's a story about friendship." "Then you need to go back and write it that way." She went on to remind me that in any true friendship both friends change and grow because they know each other. "I see how Jesse has changed because he has known Leslie, but I don't see how knowing Jesse has changed Leslie. How has Jesse made a difference in her life?"

That was the problem that had to be solved to turn my pitiful little cry of anguish into a real story. And as I pondered it, up from the dust of the playground at Calvin H. Wiley School arose Pansy and her two gigantic cohorts who had bullied me when I was a fourth grader. It would be Pansy alias Janice Avery who would show how Jesse's friendship enriched Leslie's life.

I revised *Bridge to Terabithia* extensively and it was published. It was and is a simple story, told in only 128 pages, and the first edition, as I recall, was a modest seven thousand copies. At the time, I wondered if anyone who was not named Paterson would understand it at all. I am still astounded by the response to the book, more than thirty-five years later. But here I want to tell you what it taught me as a writer who was so afraid of mediocrity that she almost didn't dare to become a writer at all.

As children, as adolescents, and even, I fear, as adults, most of us are afraid that if we reveal ourselves as we really are to one another, we will be despised. In writing *Bridge to Terabithia*, I went into the deepest, darkest regions of myself and offered it to my readers, and my readers, through the years, have given the deepest parts of their own souls to my book and together we have created, across barriers of age and race and religion and nationality—even across language barriers—a deep human connection, which in a world torn apart by divisions seems miraculous to me.

At a conference once, a woman said, "I think it's wonderful how open you are." I was quite startled. "You don't understand," I said, "writers are very private people . . . who run around naked in public." So when I think of writing, I really think first of the trip inward. What is it that I care so deeply and passionately about that I want to share it with that wonderful person, my reader? Am I willing to run around naked in public—to lay bare my own mind and heart and spirit to share this passion? Can I forget who might not approve or who might want me to go in a different direction? Am I determined to be as plainly honest as I can be in telling this story?

But of course there is another step—my early drafts of *Bridge to Terabithia* were simply a cry of pain from the depths. They were not yet a story—the chaos within must be brought into the light of day and be shaped by all the art at our disposal before it will speak a coherent word to another person, much less become a dancing star.

Perhaps the story I'm going to tell next belongs in the chapter I have called "Motherhood (Less than Ideal)," because the seed of *The Great Gilly Hopkins* certainly grew out of that thorny ground.

It began in the spring of 1975. I was recovering physically

and writing *Bridge to Terabithia,* while on the other side of the world all hell had broken loose. South Vietnam fell and then Cambodia. My children were watching the dreadful news on television and were upset by scenes of the children who were victims of the disasters. They had been nagging me for another brother or sister since Mary got out of diapers, so now they were begging me to adopt some of these homeless children. And I was saying, "I can't take care of more than four children. We can't afford any more children." We compromised. We wouldn't adopt any more, but we would provide temporary foster care for any child that came to the Washington area if asked. Since Lutheran Social Service had certified John and me as genuine okay parents when we adopted Mary, I offered them our services. We were asked to take in two Cambodian boys for two weeks while the immigration authorities figured out what to do with a planeload of Cambodian children that had arrived at Dulles Airport with no identification other than name tags hanging around their necks.

That seemed manageable to me. We bought bunk beds for the boys' room, and I started cooking rice three times a day, thinking how lucky these boys were to land in the home of a woman who knew how to cook rice properly. Needless to say, it wasn't as easy as cooking rice as the two weeks stretched into two more weeks and two more and yet more. The honeymoon period when all six children were behaving was quickly over. I learned a lot about children, about being a foster parent, and especially about myself that, given the choice, I'd just as soon not have learned. Up until then I had thought of myself as a B– or at least C+ mother, and now as a foster mother I was flunking.

I had to ask myself why, and I found my answer in my own mind. When I met each of our four children, either in the delivery room or at the airport, I knew this child was mine—that there was no backing out for either of us. For better or worse, in sickness and in health, we would belong to each other as parent and child as long as we both lived.

This sort of conviction does something to a relationship, and both you and the child know it. When problems arise, there is no escape, so you try to work them out. But with these boys, I would find myself thinking, *I can't really deal with that. They'll be here such a short time.* Or, *Thank heavens they'll soon be gone.* What I was doing was treating two human beings as though they were disposable. That's why crimes are committed. That's why wars are fought. Because someone thinks someone else is disposable.

Writers tend to write a book to answer their own questions. My question was: How would I feel if the world regarded me as disposable? And I decided I would be very angry. After the book was published, I realized, belatedly, that I had put two foster children in the story. I might not have been Gilly. I might well have been William Ernest. Although I love to perform, I am shy in social situations like publishers' cocktail parties and church coffee hours. When I feel that people are treating me as though I'm disposable,

I want to disappear, and I would, if Maime Trotter's broad back were available for me to hide behind.

I'm better now that I'm old, but I've had to work to become less shy. I've had to think of all the other people in the room who are probably just as shy as I am.

Jean Little, Claire Mackay, and me.

Dedications and Other Miscellanea

If you've read this far, you will know that my first five books were dedicated to my husband and four children. As in-laws came into the family, they got books, as have the grandchildren, including our "adopted" grandchild, Kate Greene. My terrific sisters were cited in *The Same Stuff as Stars,* as was my brother's widow. My first collection of Christmas stories, *Angels and Other Strangers,* remembers my parents. My mother died before it was published, but I was able to tell her about the inscription, which also includes

Takoma Park Presbyterian Church, where the stories were first read aloud. The second volume, *A Midnight Clear*, was for the two congregations that heard those stories. Husband John is also honored in *The Tale of the Mandarin Ducks*, which started out as an exercise for How to Use a Computer and then became an anniversary present.

Teachers and librarians have enriched my life, and my books of essays were for four of my great teachers, and *Bread and Roses, Too* was for Karen Lane, who is the kind of librarian every town should have. I wrote of Barbara Thompson in an earlier chapter, and if you see her name linked with Hazel Horton's in *Marvin One Too Many*, it is because both of them have spent their lives as exemplary teachers of the very young. Hazel was my college roommate and also remains a dear friend. She is from the Appalachian hills and used to sing the old songs that are echoed in *Come Sing, Jimmy Jo*.

I dedicated *Jacob Have I Loved* to Gene Namovicz. I was trying to be a bit clever with it, saying I wish it were *Emma* (a Jane Austen we both loved). People of my generation know the famous quotation from Helen Hayes's autobiography about the peanuts that Charles McArthur put in her hand, saying, "I wish they were emeralds." Gene would have rather had a good book any day than emeralds.

Rebels of the Heavenly Kingdom is my thanks to Virginia Buckley. No one ever had a better editor, and since the book was set in China, I thought a Chinese saying was appropriate: "A thousand thoughts; ten thousand thanks," though ten thousand would still be far too few. Lauren Wohl, one of the great library promotion people I have worked with, has the distinction of being the dedicatee of both the authors and the illustrator for *Consider the Lilies.*

With the dedicatee of *Come Sing, Jimmy Jo* I have the longest history. Mary Watt Sorum's mother and my mother were friends at the General Assembly's Training School before her mother went to the Belgian Congo and my mother went to China. We can't remember a time when we didn't know about each other. If, as children, we whined, Mother would remind us that Georgia Watt's children in Africa all had polio and she had TB. Whereas when the Watt children whined, their mother would tell them how Mary Goetchius's children were running away from war and occupation. You'd think that would make Mary and me never want to meet, but meet we did when we were both teenagers. We knew that first day that we would be friends for life and we are.

Jean Little and her dear friend and mine Claire Mackay got a book. Jean, who is often referred to as "Canada's most beloved writer for children," recently recalled an interviewer who asked what she wanted to be called. "Why, Jean Little," she said, a bit surprised by the question. "No," he said, "I mean, do you want to be called 'visually challenged' or—" "How about blind?" she said. "Oh, no," said the shocked interviewer, "*they* don't like to

Virginia Buckley, my editor for forty years.

be called that." I once went to England as Jean's seeing-eye dog. I am proud to say that I was quite a good one and laughed louder at her stories than the actual dog or dogs ever did.

Ted and Alice Vial were our dearest friends from Princeton Seminary days. At nine and a half months, John Jr. took his first steps on their living room floor. Grace Greene and Nancy Graff of *Jip, His Story* are chief among the many friends who have made Vermont feel like my real home. In her introduction, Nancy has already told you about our weekly lunches at Wayside that continue to be more important to me than she will ever know, and Grace, the mother of our adopted grandchild, starred in chapter one.

Stephanie Tolan and I have waged peace together as well as co-written four plays, three of which we collaborated on with Steve Liebman. With few of my long-time friends have I shared more joys and grief than with Kathryn Morton, to whom I dedicated *Park's Quest*. *The Day of the Pelican* is dedicated to the Kosovar family that inspired it and to Mark Ofila, whose knowledge and love of Kosova made it possible for me to write the story. Margaret Mahy was a writer both John and I admired extravagantly, as well a cherished friend. Steven and Helen Kellogg have brightened our lives for more than a quarter of a century. The three of them share the page in *The Flint Heart,* a book wonderfully illustrated by John Rocco. Mary Brigid Barrett is the incomparable President of the National Children's Book and Literacy Alliance, and she and her whole family are an inspiration as well as just plain fun to be with. I felt this family of artists needed a truly beautiful book, and when I saw Pamela Dalton's exquisite paper-cut illustrations for *Brother Sun, Sister Moon* I knew it must be inscribed for them. Christopher Franceschelli was the publisher of that book and also much earlier at Dutton, the publisher of *Parzival: The Quest of the Grail Knight,* my re-telling of Wolfram von Eschenbach's epic poem, which I dedicated to him.

Any of these wonderful friends is worthy of a book, but it's like that T-shirt. She wrote a whole book and all I got was this lousy line. And some people, who have been really important to me, didn't even get a line. I beg forgiveness of them all.

Accepting the Wilder from Martha Parravano, chair of the committee.

Awards, Etc.

People often ask about awards, and there are always stories surrounding such events. When *The Master Puppeteer* was nominated for the National Book Award, Sophie Silberberg called from Thomas Y. Crowell to tell me. She told me not to worry about winning, as just to be nominated was honor enough, but that since the award would be given in three days, it would be a good idea to prepare a five-hundred-word acceptance speech just in case one would be needed. There was no way I was going to write a speech for a prize I wasn't going to win, so when Sophie called with the unbelievable news that I had actually won, I was, of course, unprepared.

John Sr. was out of town. (It is a rule of nature that spouses are always out of town when they are most needed.) It was a school holiday, and Lin and John had taken off on their bikes with several friends for a ride to a park in Silver Spring where they planned to have a picnic lunch. While I was still trying to recover from Sophie's call, the telephone rang. This time it was a woman telling me that there had been a bike accident involving my daughter. One of the children in the outing had gone to her house and asked her to call me.

There was no more thought of the award or of any speech. I hopped in the car and raced to the address the woman had given me. After I made sure Lin was fine, though her bicycle wasn't rideable, I told her and John the news and that I had to write five hundred deathless words by evening, so that Sophie and Virginia Buckley could vet them and turn them over to the press the next morning. I drove Lin and her broken bike home and set to work. I promised the children that if they would leave me alone for the entire afternoon I would take them to supper at any restaurant they chose and they could order anything they wanted.

With such an offer, they happily complied. I mean, at that point in our lives, going to a fast-food place and splitting the hamburgers in half was "going out for dinner." I think it was well after six before Sophie and Virginia agreed that the speech

Virginia Buckley and me at the National Book Awards for The Master Puppeteer 1977.

was okay, and the children and I could go out and celebrate. They chose a new place that served the usual hamburger fare, but was noted for monster ice cream dishes. It was very loud and ordinary, but I didn't care. We were a happy bunch. Suddenly, I was aware that our booth was surrounded by the entire waitstaff singing: "For she's a jolly good fellow," at the end of which they shouted in unison: "Congratulations to Katherine Paterson, the greatest children's writer in the world!"

Even in that noisy restaurant, heads were turning. My face was red, but my smug children were beaming.

The prize for winning the National Book Award in 1977 was one thousand dollars—more undesignated cash than my family had ever seen, so it seemed to me that it shouldn't go for beans or bills. I asked the children what they would like to do with the prize money. With one voice they voted to go to Busch Gardens, an amusement park that had just opened near Williamsburg, Virginia. Now, I do not like crowds or rides; therefore, an amusement park would be my *last* choice on where to spend prize money, but I'd asked, and this was their choice.

The motel had a swimming pool. At this point in our lives, we hadn't frequented motels. It never occurred to me that I should have packed swim gear. The sign at the pool strictly forbade swimming in unsuitable gear, but it was hot, and I had four children panting to leap into the water. Heck, I'd just won the National Book Award. What could they do if my kids swam in shorts and T-shirts, sue me? "Go ahead," I said. "Jump in!" I felt reckless and gleeful, flaunting the rules.

The next day was one of the hardest days of motherhood. I had to avert my eyes as my precious children rode and re-rode the most terrifying thrill rides I had ever imagined. Their father even took a ride or two. I sat huddled over a table in the shade trying not to look. Near the end of the day, Mary was delegated to make sure I had some fun. She decided to take me on the baby roller coaster—the one they let wee children ride. I hated every stomach-churning minute of it.

When we were at last safely in the car, I was breathing normally but the children were still giddy from their great day. "When can we do this again?" they demanded. I wanted to say "Never," but I said what I thought was the same thing: "The next time I win the National Book Award." Two years later when *Gilly* won, they reminded me of my promise. I made their father take them. I stayed at home, where there was no chance that I might inadvertently see what they were daring to ride or how often.

Years ago, my friend Phyllis Naylor made a speech in which she said: "Katherine Paterson and I discovered that we share a certain neurosis, which is this: As long as we are being rejected, ignored, and unreviewed, we prove ourselves strong and tenacious and resilient. The harder the wind blows, the taller we stand. We're sad, of course, but *strong*. Let some success blow our way, however, and while we are, of course, happy, we're terrified, dyspeptic, and sleepless."

So what happens to a writer who has lived out a comfortable fourteen-odd years of genteel failure and modest attention, only to be suddenly pronounced an overnight success? Or, how does it feel, Mrs. Paterson, to win the National Book Award in 1977, the Newbery Medal in 1978, the National Book Award and Newbery Honor in 1979, and the Newbery Medal in 1981? Well, as I said earlier, I felt like Job backwards. "Why me, Lord? Why me?" These days I'm grateful, not worthy, but *very* grateful. At the beginning, it cost me more stomach churning than catching a glimpse of my children screaming with glee atop Die Wildkatze roller coaster in Busch Gardens.

On the morning of Wednesday, January 25 at 5:49 a.m., the phone rang. My husband gave a sleepy grunt and handed it to me. On the other end an incredibly wide-awake voice gave me the news that *Bridge to Terabithia* had won the Newbery Medal. Peter Spier, the Caldecott winner, said his wife went down and got the leftover New Year's champagne. John went down to the kitchen and brought me up a cup of warm milk.

I had been directed not to tell anyone, but to take a plane on Thursday and come to Chicago for the official announcement. I had promised to speak in a Baltimore school on Thursday morning. Would I need to lie to the librarian friend who had invited me? I called and as soon as I said I would need to postpone my visit, she cried: "That's wonderful!" Apparently, she knew without being told the reason.

When I got up the next morning, John was already up with the radio on. "Chicago doesn't look too good," he said. It was something of an understatement. I had made a twelve noon reservation in order to get there by the 4:30 press conference. I rushed to the airport to get the ten o'clock flight. No one told me that the twelve had already been canceled and the eight a.m. was still in a holding pattern over the Midwest. I settled myself in the seat for the trip, my usual jitters quiet. I felt bathed in a warm orange glow—the kind you feel when you know that you love and are loved in return. Ah, I thought, this is how it feels to win the Newbery.

My warm glow sputtered out sometime during the endless

circles over O'Hare. It began to dawn on me that I might not get there for the 4:30 press conference and subsequent celebration. What will they do? Surely they couldn't go on without me. I was dead wrong. They not only could go on without me, they did. More than one person assured me it was the best party they remembered. Peter Spier, the only winner and honor recipient to get there, single-handedly charmed the press and the American Library Association, melting the heart of blizzard-bound Chicago, while I sat in Kansas City frantic because a phone call to HarperCollins let me know that my editor Virginia had left New York at the same time I had left Washington, and she hadn't been heard from since. I knew I could go on writing books without a medal, but I darkly suspected that without Virginia, I was finished. On Friday afternoon I stumbled into National Airport, ready to kiss the carpet. Virginia was okay and I was home. It didn't matter if I got a prize or not.

As the days went by, it all seemed less and less real. I fully expected another phone call with the voice at the other end saying; "Now that you've had your fun, the real Newbery Medal goes to . . ." Then one day a long envelope arrived in the mail. Inside were ten gold seals. Engraved on the seals were the familiar words that had blinked at me seductively since those days I was a library helper at Calvin H. Wiley Elementary School. It was there that I discovered Kate Seredy, Robert Lawson, and Rachel Field. And here were those same gold stickers, ready for me to peel off and stick to the jacket of a book with my name on it.

It is amazing how quickly one becomes accustomed to glory. I began to admire my own copy of *Bridge to Terabithia* with its new seal. I held it up so the light from the dining room window could bounce off of it. There was no one home to share it with except our dog Blossom and she was not interested. I needed to show it off. It was my proof that I had actually won the same medal Kate and Robert and Rachel had won so many years before. I mean, they wouldn't have sent me the seals if they were really going to give the medal to someone else, now would they?

At last the children came trooping home from school. "Look!" I cried. "Look what came in the mail!" They had all been so thrilled when the news first came, but now they looked dutifully at the seal and headed for the kitchen. "What's for snack?" "Isn't it beautiful?" I said. "This gold seal is going to be on every copy of *Bridge to Tera-bithia* that's ever printed!" "Brag. Brag. Brag," said my ten-year-old Mary. Back in the real world, I helped them assemble their snacks.

I gave myself a gift when *Bridge* won. I decided that we were now rich enough to buy fresh milk. "I will never mix another gallon of dried skim milk as long as I live," I promised myself, and I haven't. When *Jacob Have I Loved* won in 1981 we had just moved to Norfolk and I was homesick for my Washington-area friends. My gift to myself that time was that I could call my friends long-distance whenever I wanted to. I still do that.

At the Newbery banquet in 1978, John was sitting on the platform with me, but the four children were seated at the table squarely in front of the podium with the Harper crowd. I asked

At the Newbery banquet for Bridge, 1978.

Lin and Mary at the Newbery, 1978.

The Paterson kids whooping it up in San Francisco with Bill Morris and Lauren Wohl at 1981 Newbery for Jacob Have I Loved.

Lauren Wohl to sit by David because I was afraid my relating the story of Lisa's death might be very hard for him. Lauren tells the story that as the speech went on, she was the one sobbing, and David was handing her a Kleenex and saying, "Are you all right? Are you all right?"

People often ask me which is my favorite book, and, I, like many other writers, feel as though I'm being asked to choose a favorite child. I don't think any of them (books or children) are perfect and I love them all. I have a different relationship with each one, so it would be impossible to compare them on the basis of who or which is the favorite. But when I'm asked which book I'm proud-est of, I say, "*Jacob Have I Loved.*" There are several reasons I'm proud of *Jacob*. When *The Master Puppeteer* won the NBA, I had already finished writing *Bridge*. When *Bridge* won the Newbery, *Gilly* was about to be published. But when *Gilly* received both the NBA and Newbery Honor, I was in the early struggling stages with *Jacob*. How could this pitiful little non-book compete? I was terrified that it would die before it had a chance to be born. Or if I finished it, it would be published no matter how awful it was (in those days that fragment *was* truly awful) and my career and reputation would collapse into ruins.

I thought about trying to finish it and then sending it to Virginia anonymously in a plain brown wrapper—no email submissions in those days. If she read it and liked it without any medal-heavy author's name on it, then I would go ahead and let it be published. If she rejected it, I would know the truth. In a telephone call that spring she asked me if I was working. I said that I was trying to, but I wasn't sure if it was any good or not, so she might not ever see it. "Well, just promise me you won't send it to me anonymously," she said. I never told her that I had thought of doing just that.

My mother died in February just after *Gilly* was announced as the Newbery Honor book and before it won the NBA. We moved from Takoma Park, where we had spent thirteen wonderful years, to Norfolk just before she died. So I lost my mother and all my Washington-area friends at the same time. The only thing that kept me from drowning with grief that year was my struggle with *Jacob*. I had decided on the Jacob and Esau theme when I'd heard several of my delightful, intelligent friends talk about the way they still carried the psychic wounds of childhood. "Mother always loved him best," said one. "If my sister hadn't stolen my doll when I was seven years old . . ." began another. *Do you really want to live your life crippled by your envy of your brother?* I wondered. *Isn't there some statute of limitations on what your sister did when you were seven?*

Since I have grown up with Biblical stories, I began to look at the sibling relationships in those stories. Cain commits murder because he is jealous of his brother Abel. Jacob steals his brother's birthright and his brother Esau wants to kill him. Jacob's two wives are sisters, and the older one is envious of her younger sister because she knows that Jacob loves Rachel best. And on it goes. *I will write about this,* I thought, *it's a universal theme.* I didn't think it was my own problem until I sat down to write, but every time I sat down at my desk I was so filled with fury that I could hardly type. Hmmm. Someone else's problem? Maybe not. As I've often said, writing is a lot cheaper than psychotherapy.

When I was trying to figure the story out, when I was expending all kinds of fierce anger (as I first thought) at Louise for not realizing how much her parents and sister loved her, I was in the world of my book—not the world of sorrow and loneliness that I woke up to every morning. It seemed an impossible task, this book of blind jealousy that was making me furious. I tried desperately to write it, as I had all the previous novels, in the third person, but Louise's voice kept intruding. She demanded the story be told her way. "All right," I told her, "you can have the first draft. Next time I'll fix it." But the voice persisted into every attempt I made at third person. I finally realized that Louise is so consumed with envy she cannot see anyone else's viewpoint. "But you are writing for young people," some have said, "how can you trust them to realize that Louise is an unreliable narrator?" Well, I do trust my young readers. They have proven themselves to be quite sophisticated. I've had more trouble with adult readers not understanding the book than with young ones.

I was walking past the phone that winter morning at about nine when it began to ring. "Katherine," a familiar voice said, "this is Ginny Kruse." "Oh, Ginny," I said, "I'm so glad you called. I've never heard from that person in Wisconsin who asked me to speak and I need to get the details . . ." She broke in abruptly. "Katherine, I'm not calling about that. I'm calling to tell you that *Jacob Have I Loved* has won the 1981 Newbery Medal." "You've got to be kidding," I said. After all, I already had my medal. "I wouldn't kid about something like this," she said a bit sternly.

The original six at the Ambassador for Young People's Literature ceremony at the Library of Congress, January 2010.

This time it went much more smoothly. Winners were being called during normal waking hours and no one was expected to fly in for a press conference—just show up in June for the big celebration. Bill Morris, the legendary library promotion director at Harper, called to congratulate me and fill me in on the details. "We want the whole family to come again," he said. "Bill, you know how big my family is. One husband, four children." Yes, of course, he knew, and they were all to come to San Francisco.

But my children were three years older and less naive than they had been when *Bridge* won the Newbery. On the night before the Newbery/Caldecott, we had been invited to a lovely dinner in a San Francisco home. The children opted out. They had discovered room service and thought they'd eat in and maybe watch TV or something. It seemed quite reasonable. By now Lin was eighteen and John seventeen and both quite responsible young adults.

We got back to the hotel soon after ten o'clock to find thirteen-year-old Mary alone in the room, weeping heartbrokenly. She finally got out the fact that after dinner the older three had decided to go out and see a movie. She didn't want to leave the hotel—after all, they had said they'd stay in and watch TV—but the older three had promised they'd be home right after the movie. *And they'd never come back.* She was quite sure all her siblings had been killed or left for dead on the streets of the city.

We tried to reassure her, but it was hard to reassure ourselves. If they'd gone right after supper to a movie, they should have been back long ago. Eleven o'clock went by, and then twelve with no return. The way I've gotten through motherhood is to recite the motto: *Panic at the last possible moment.* As the clock crept toward one, the last possible moment seemed nearly upon me. Should I call the desk? The police? Area hospitals? What could anyone do? If three of my children were dead or injured, would they insist that I go ahead with my speech that night?

It was almost one o'clock when they came in laughing. The first show had been full, they said, so they bought tickets for the next. Then when they came out, they couldn't find a taxi, so they walked back. They couldn't believe anyone would worry. They were fine. Well, their parents and their little sister were wrecks, but we recovered. Recovered, that is, until I checked out and saw the room service bill. I was totally appalled and humiliated. I apologized profusely to Bill Morris, who, ever the gentleman, said it was fine—not to worry. A few years later he told me that the MacLachlan kids had beat out the Paterson kids for most room service orders. Patty and I are both able to laugh about it now.

It was the spring of 1998 and I was aware that sometime soon, the Hans Christian Andersen winners would be announced. I was at Calvin College for their biennial festival of Faith and Writing, where I was to be one of the three keynote speakers. I remember standing at a window in Gary Schmidt's guest house realizing that although I had been nominated for a third time, there was little likelihood that I would ever win the award, and suddenly, it was all right. It didn't matter, but late that very afternoon a call came telling me that I had indeed won. The Andersen is an international prize that gives its winners a sort of ambassadorial status to the children's literature community in more than seventy member countries. I would be relating with persons from diverse cultures and religions, speaking many languages. There would be Israelis and Palestinians. There would be Russians and Chinese and Iranians. There would be citizens of African nations and islands of the Pacific. I was at that moment overwhelmed with gratitude. I felt somehow that God trusted me with this mission. It was an amazing feeling.

We went to dinner but I could hardly eat, and after dinner we went to the jam-packed gymnasium to hear the first keynote speaker, Elie Wiesel.

I was seated just below the dais and I watched and listened to what I will always believe was the greatest talk on the relation of faith to writing that I had ever heard. He strode back and forth on the platform, with no notes whatsoever, telling of his life from the concentration camp whose horrors robbed him of words to his finally being able to find words for the unspeakable.

I lay in bed that night, unable to sleep. Of course, I was still feeling the thrill of the Andersen announcement, but I could hardly enjoy it for wondering how I could possibly get up before that same audience the next night. How could anyone? The speech that I had worked on so long seemed childish and inadequate at best. How could I dare deliver it after Elie Wiesel's earth-shattering presentation? But there was no escape. My name was on the posters all over town. And then I had an inspiration, and if you're me, you'd call it divine.

This is what I said when I got up before that crowd the next night. "The name of my talk is 'Image and Imagination,' and I want to begin with an imaginative exercise. Take out a piece of paper [and here I made a rectangle with my hands roughly 18 x 24] about this size—" I could see some of the women scrabbling about in their large purses, so I said: "No, no, this is an *imaginative* exercise. Okay. Now on that paper, down here in the right-hand corner I want you to print in bold block letters: 'Elie Wiesel.' And here a bit lower, print 'John Updike,' and right between them, put your own name." There was a moment of puzzled silence and then a roar of laughter at which point I said: "Now that I have your complete sympathy, I'll begin my talk."

One last story. I was awakened at six a.m. on a March morning by a phone call from Sweden telling me that I was to be the 2006 winner of the Astrid Lindgren Memorial Award. This award of five million krona is given each year by the Swedish people to honor the memory of their most beloved writer for children. As soon as they heard the news, my children announced the whole family was coming to Sweden whether invited or not. So from that first morning until we actually left for Stockholm on the 26th of May, my five-year-old granddaughter could talk of nothing but the fact that she was going to meet a real princess. Her mother and I were a bit apprehensive. We knew that

Crown Princess Victoria was slated to be at the award ceremonies, but we had no idea what the security measures would be, much less what the protocol was for meeting the future crowned head of Sweden. Jordan was busy practicing her curtsey, but when I asked Larry Lempert, the chair of the jury, how I should greet the princess, he said, "Oh, give her a high five."

Needless to say, I sought other advice, and I was told simply to follow her lead. "She's very down-to-earth," everyone said. "She'll probably offer to shake hands." Which is exactly what she did.

Before the day of the actual prize giving, I spoke to groups of children and adults and was interviewed on and on by every segment of the media imaginable. I gave a long, formal speech the night before the big event, because the event itself was to be for the enjoyment of children. It took place in a huge outdoor amphitheater so there would be plenty of room for whole families to come. There were a couple of very short speeches—mine that day took less than two minutes—the rest of the program consisted of popular entertainment children were sure to enjoy. (My grandchildren went around afterward getting autographs from the singers, rappers, dancers, and acrobats who performed—not from me—well, not until I asked them if they'd like the winner's signature on their programs as well.)

The princess and I were comfortably seated in chairs with our backs to the huge audience a few minutes before the festivities began. She was just as down-to-earth as all her subjects had promised me she would be, so I felt free to mention that my grandchildren were eager to meet her and to ask if that would be possible. "Of course," she said, "but why don't we wait for the photographers so they can have their pictures taken?"

I thought that was a great idea, but somehow, each of my seven grandchildren from ages four through sixteen found he or she had something to say to their grandmother that couldn't possibly wait until after the ceremony. They all made their way down from their seats in the audience to speak to me, so, quite naturally, I had to introduce them to the princess, who shook hands with each one, asked their names, and greeted them all as cordially as if they had been a friendly diplomatic delegation.

Of course, when the paparazzi lined up to take pictures afterward, my seven grandchildren were right there again to have themselves photographed with their old pal, Her Royal Highness.

Jordan, especially, was thrilled. When the photography session ended, she asked her mother, "*Now* are we famous?" Samantha assured her she was. She skipped over to me and happily took my hand to walk to the restaurant on the grounds where the reception for all the famous people in attendance was being held.

When we went in, there on the table where guests were being checked in was the same picture of her grandmother that had been on the front page of the newspaper and posted on the stage and in various sites around the city. We started up the stairs and there at the top of the stairs was yet another picture of her grandmother—this one nearly the size of her own front door. She took one look, sighed deeply, and began to shake her head. "Nana. Nana. Nana," she said.

"Are you tired of Nana, Jordan?" I asked.

"Yessss."

Enough said.

John and Annie.

Final Gifts

I had thought that this book was finished. I had mailed off revisions to Kate Harrison, the editor, and was gathering pictures to include with the text when I was interrupted by the most extraordinary story of my life.

This story began, as all stories seem to, years before. I noticed one day that my strong, athletic husband was shuffling his feet when he walked. "John," I said, "pick up your feet. You're

283

walking like your father did when he was ninety years old." I was laughing when I said it, but I had no way of knowing what was happening. In time, and after extensive tests, doctors at Dartmouth Hospital concluded that John had a rare neurological disorder called multiple systems atrophy, for which there is no known cure. A small mountain of medications and a variety of therapies, occupational and physical, are prescribed with the hope that something might help, or at least slow down the progress of the disease, but the hard truth of the matter is that nothing can halt it.

John was a fine tennis player, he even won a varsity letter at Swarthmore, a competitive college for tennis as well as academics. But not too long after I had noticed the shuffling walk, he realized that he was no longer up to the speed and particularly the balance that tennis demanded. An even greater blow came when he failed a mandatory driver's exam and could no longer hop into his car and go wherever he wished. Then he needed a cane, a walker, and finally a wheelchair. "I don't mind dying," he said more than once, "but I don't want to die by inches." But that was exactly what was happening to every part of his body bit by bit. The man who had spent his life helping others had a very hard time being the one in need of constant care. He had promised on the day he proposed that he would help me, but now he could only think of himself as a burden.

One very bright spot in this increasingly dark scenario was the time we spent doing the abridgment of *The Flint Heart* together.

John had fallen in love with the early twentieth-century book, now long out of print, and Karen Lotz at Candlewick encouraged us to try to make it accessible for twenty-first-century children.

John went through the original chapter by chapter and noted what was essential to telling the story and what would make any modern reader pitch the hefty volume across the room. I would go upstairs and cut and paste and rewrite and bring it back down for him to approve. I knew he needed to keep on being creative, and was delighted that he went on to write a short picture book about a boy who makes a kaleidoscope. He found two persons who would translate the story into French and Spanish, and our friend Kitty Werner found an illustrator and helped John publish his three-language book especially for children learning another language and even adult ESL students. But in another year, the man who once had been tested with an IQ that would have qualified him to join Mensa had great difficulty playing bridge, his favorite card game. He wouldn't be writing any more books; in fact, as the months wore on, he was no longer able to write his name in one.

After my two-year term as the National Ambassador for Young People's Literature, I cut back on out of town trips. It was hard to find good caregivers to take over in my absence. At home, there was less and less time or energy for writing.

We have many supportive friends, but I needed more help. First it was three days a week, then five, then three nights, four nights, until at last it was someone in addition to me twenty-four hours

285

a day. John was losing an alarming amount of weight, nothing tasted good, getting a fork or spoon to his mouth was a challenge, and he was obviously having difficulty swallowing.

On my 2013 fall schedule there were only two events. I went to the first of these, probably my favorite event, the National Book Festival in DC. On Sunday morning I called the weekend caregiver—John had had a rough night but everything was fine now. I spoke briefly to John and he seemed to be as okay as things were at that time. I went on to the mall for the day's events. However, within forty-five minutes of our phone conversation, the weekend caregiver had called Stephen, our wonderful five-day-a-week caregiver. Zia was worried about John, would Stephen come over and see what he thought?

John was listless and having difficulty breathing. Stephen felt that they should take John to the emergency room. By the time Stephen was able to reach me in DC, the three of them were already at the hospital. I asked Stephen if I should cancel my two commitments for the day and try to get a flight as soon as possible. "No," he said. "We don't know anything yet. They're checking him over. I'll let you know when we know something."

The next call I got was from the emergency room doctor who said that John had double pneumonia and they would be admitting him to intensive care. While I carried out my duties at the festival, a young Library of Congress staffer got me an earlier flight back to Vermont. I stopped at the hospital on my way back from the airport. John was sleeping peacefully, hooked up to every device available in a well-equipped ICU unit. His color was good and he seemed better than he'd been for a long time. Although John had tried to make me promise over the last couple of years that I wouldn't ever take him to the hospital again, I was grateful that Stephen had chosen to take him there. I went home and slept well.

When I went back the next morning, the young doctor on duty came in the room to see us both. He spoke in a very caring manner, but he spoke frankly. Perhaps with the massive dose of antibiotics they were giving John, they might be able to cure this bout of pneumonia, he said, but they couldn't cure the MSA, which would result in continuous bouts of pneumonia, each one more debilitating until he was too weak to recover. You need to think, he said, how you want to spend the rest of your life. By Tuesday afternoon, tests confirmed that 64 percent of what John was swallowing was going to his lungs. Yes, it was possible to insert a feeding tube into the stomach, but those were liable to infections and the doctor really didn't recommend it. You are in charge, he told John. If you want us to keep treating you, we will, but if you decide you'd rather go home with hospice care, we can promise you that we will keep you comfortable while "nature takes its course."

The hospital's palliative care nurse came in frequently. She was equally caring and truthful about John's options. It occurred to me that these honest, compassionate people were what was being called the "death squad" by persons opposed to the affordable care act.

Now, it is one thing, we learned, as you lose one vital ability after another to say, "Why doesn't God just take me?" but it is another when the option is presented and it becomes your decision. John thought about it, slept on it, and on Wednesday morning, looked at me as though he were my child and not my husband. "What do you advise?" he asked.

"Oh, sweetie," I said. "I want you to live as long as you can, but I don't want you to be miserable."

"I want to go home," he said. And then, "I'll miss you."

By now I was sobbing. "I'll miss you too." Then I remembered a story. The day before Ray died, his pastor and close friend had said to him, "Ray, when you get there, will you promise to prepare a place for me?" And Ray had promised he would. So I reminded John of this story and asked him to prepare a place for me. He smiled and seemed satisfied. The man who always wanted to do things for me (whether I wanted him to or not) had one more gigantic task to do for me.

From that time on, John seemed to be at complete peace with his decision, even telling his favorite nurse that she would be notified about the memorial service in case she could come.

I called the family to tell them that we were going home. David had come on Wednesday, and Lin called and asked if she should come as well. "I don't know how long it will be," I said. But she knew better than I. She called the others to assemble in Vermont that weekend.

We went home on Thursday. David had hung a number of

John's glassworks in the window where John would be able to see them best. He and Stephen Casadonte met the medical supply van with the hospital bed, the suction pump, and oxygen machine. Everything went into the living room so there would be a comfortable place for visitors. The hospice nurses came with the medications to keep him comfortable and showed me how to administer them. "You're a good scout," he whispered once as I put a few drops of morphine into his mouth.

On their first visit, one of the nurses gave me a copy of a book entitled *Final Gifts*. The book was written by two hospice nurses who had been inspired by the gifts dying persons can give the living if the living are open to receiving them. One thing the book alerted me to was that the dying often speak in a coded language and the living should be ready for that.

Friday morning John asked if the mail had come. "Not yet," I said. "You remember they've put Todd [our longtime carrier] on a different route and the new person doesn't come as early as he used to." Then I remembered what the book had said and did an about-face. "Why? Were you expecting something?"

"No," he said. "It's for you."

"What is it?" I asked.

"It's a special message."

"What does the message say?"

He looked at me indignantly. "I don't open your mail."

"It's all right. I give you permission."

But that was the end of the conversation. The special message was something I was going to have to open myself.

There was more laughter that week than I would have imagined. On Saturday morning, for example, I was in the living room when our son John came in and sat near the bed. He made an elaborate show of looking all around the room. "Okay, Dad," he said. "There's no one else around, you can tell me. Aren't I your favorite child?" His father didn't even bother to open his eyes. "No comment," he said.

Later that morning, John said: "Where is the dog?" I found Pixie and brought her in. Then he said, "Tell everyone to come in."

I summoned the children—including David's wife, Aviana Tadler, and Lin's husband, Stephen Pierce, all of whom were busy cleaning house—into the living room. Like a king from his throne John told them how much he loved them and how grateful he was for them. Son-in-law Stephen took a beautiful picture right afterward of John surrounded by his family. We all look amazingly happy. One by one each child then went in and had a private word with their father. Afterward, the hospice nurse said to him, "You know, John, you don't have to worry. Katherine and the children are going to be fine."

"Good," he said. I don't remember that he said anything else after that.

He opened his eyes Sunday afternoon when his youngest grandchild came to say good-bye, but he didn't speak. His beloved adopted granddaughter Katie Greene came in with her parents a little later. I feel sure he knew they were there, but he was no longer able to respond. When the hospice nurse came in on Monday morning she expressed surprise at the dramatic change in John's body from the day before. The children had all gone home on Sunday, but I called our daughter Mary, who lives in Vermont, and told her that the nurse didn't think her father would live more than twenty-four or forty-eight hours. She came that afternoon. I called the agency to cancel the night person. Stephen Casadonte wanted to stay on, and he was the only caregiver we wanted with us. At about nine, our pastors, Carl and Gina Hilton-VanOsdall, came. They anointed John with oil and prayed with us. After they left I was sent to bed, but close to ten, both Mary and Stephen saw that John's breathing had changed dramatically, so Stephen woke me up. I came into the living room to see Mary standing on one side of his bed holding her father's right hand. I went and stood on the other side and held his left hand. For twenty minutes we watched as his breathing slowed and then quietly stopped.

The hospice bereavement counselor listened as I told her this story. "You know," she said. "Dying is hard work, and not everybody does it well. But John, who had lost control of almost every aspect of his life, took control of his own death and did a magnificent job of it."

Bit by bit, I am unwrapping John's final gift to me, the special message that I must open by myself without his help. Already I know that in his final week he gave me the most blessed week of my life and showed me in his dying that there is nothing to fear in death.

Who Went Where When

Because we always seemed to be fleeing or moving, my life and that of my family can be very confusing. So it seemed helpful to enclose a sort of time line of the events chronicled in this book.

1893 (or 1894)   George Raymond Womeldorf is born.

1895   Mary Elizabeth Goetchius is born.

1917   Raymond joins the Washington and Lee University ambulance corps.

1918   He is wounded.

1918–1920   He is in various hospitals and convalescent homes.

1920–1923   He is in Union Theological Seminary, Richmond, Virginia.

1921   Raymond and Mary meet.

1922   They get engaged.

1923   They marry and go to China for the first time.

1927   They flee to Korea.

1928   Raymond Jr. is born.

1929   Charles is born and dies at three weeks old.

1930   They return to the US on furlough and Elizabeth is born in Richmond, Virginia.

1931   They return to China.

1932   Katherine is born.

1936   Helen is born.

1937   Anne is born. The war with Japan had begun the month before.

1938   Family is evacuated to Virginia.

1939   Family returns to China and becomes friends with Maud Henderson in Shanghai. Spends the summer in Tsing Tao, moves to Ching Kiang in the fall.

1940   Family evacuated at the end of this year, again to Virginia.

1941   Move to Winston-Salem, North Carolina.

1945   World War II ends.

1946   Raymond, Mary, and four younger children leave Winston-Salem in order to return to China and are stopped at the last minute. Live for a few months in Montreat, North Carolina, and then move to Richmond, Virginia, until the fall of 1948, when they move to Charles Town, West Virginia. My parents and Helen and Anne move to Winchester, Virginia, in 1950 when there is no hope of returning to China. I go off to King College in Bristol, Tennessee and graduate in 1954.

1954–1955   I teach sixth grade in Lovettsville, Virginia, a community that is the model for Lark Creek in *Bridge to Terabithia.*

1955–1957   I attend my mother's alma mater, the General Assembly's Training School for Lay Workers in Richmond, Virginia (now a part of Union Presbyterian Seminary), where one of my professors suggests I become a writer. I don't—at least not until she gets me a job writing church school curriculum several years later.

1957–1961   I work in Japan under the Presbyterian Church US Board of World Missions.

1961–1962   I attend Union Seminary in New York City, meet John Paterson, and get married.

1963–1964   I teach at the Pennington School while John is at Princeton Seminary.

June 1964   John Jr. is born. That December Lin arrives from

295

Hong Kong, and I begin to write seriously. In 1966
David is born and in 1968 Mary arrives from the White
Mountain Apache reservation.

1966   We move to Takoma Park, Maryland, and *Who Am I?* written
for fifth- and sixth-grade Presbyterians is published.

1973   My first novel, *The Sign of the Chrysanthemum,* is published.

1974   I discover I have cancer, Lisa Hill dies, *Of Nightingales That
Weep* is published.

1975   We are temporary foster parents.

1976   *The Master Puppeteer* is published.

1977   It wins the National Book Award, and *Bridge to Terabithia* is
published.

1978   It wins the Newbery, and *The Great Gilly Hopkins* is published.

1979   It is the Newbery Honor book and wins the National Book
Award. We move to Norfolk, Virginia, and my mother dies.
Angels and Other Strangers is published.

1980   *Jacob Have I Loved* is published.

1981   It wins the Newbery, and *Gates of Excellence* and *The Crane
Wife* are published.

1983   My father dies, and *Rebels of the Heavenly Kingdom* is
published.

1985   *Come Sing, Jimmy Jo* is published.

1986   *Consider the Lilies*, John's and my first collaboration, is published, and we move to Barre, Vermont.

1987   *The Tongue-Cut Sparrow* is published.

1988   *Park's Quest* is published.

1989   *The Spying Heart* is published.

1990   *The Tale of the Mandarin Ducks* is published and wins the Boston Globe–Horn Book picture book award. The play, *Bridge to Terabithia*, by Paterson, Stephanie Tolan, and Steve Liebman premieres at Stage One, Louisville, Kentucky. Our first grandchild, Katherine Elizabeth Pierce, is born.

1991   Both *Lyddie* and my first I-Can-Read, *The Smallest Cow in the World*, are published, and I am now officially a "Vermont Author."

1992   *The King's Equal* is published, and *Who Am I?* is revised and republished.

1994   *Flip-Flop Girl* is published, and *Of Nightingales That Weep* wins the Phoenix Award for a book published twenty years before that never won a major award.

1995   *Jip, His Story, A Midnight Clear*, and the combined essay books in *A Sense of Wonder* are published.

1996   *The Angel and the Donkey* is published.

1997   *The Field of the Dogs* and *Marvin's Best Christmas Present Ever* are published.

1998   *Images of God* (with John Paterson), *Celia and the Sweet*,

Sweet Water, and *Parzival* are published, and John and I go to India, where I receive the Hans Christian Andersen Medal from the International Books for Young People.

1999   *Preacher's Boy* is published.

2000   *The Wide-Awake Princess* is published. Along with more than 70 others from politics, sports, architecture, and all the arts from music to children's literature, Judy Blume, Beverly Cleary, Maurice Sendack, and I are named "Living Legends" at the 200th birthday celebration of the Library of Congress. I go back to my home town of Huai'an, China, and have a reunion with the 1954–55 sixth grade of Lovettsville Elementary School.

2001   *The Invisible Child* and *Marvin One-Too-Many* are published.

2002   *The Same Stuff as Stars* is published.

2004   *Blueberries for the Queen* (with John Paterson) is published.

2006   *Bread and Roses, Too* is published, and our entire family of seventeen plus David's mother-in-law and Virginia and David Buckley travel to Stockholm, where I receive the Astrid Lindgren Memorial Award.

2007   Almost the entire family goes to Hollywood for the premiere of the movie *Bridge to Terabithia* that David helped write and produce. I receive the NSK Neustadt Award.

2008   *The Light of the World* is published.

2009   *The Day of the Pelican* is published and is the Vermont Reads book for the year.

2010 & 2011   I serve as Second National Ambassador for Young
              People's Literature.

2011   *Brother Sun, Sister Moon,* a reimagining of St. Francis's great
       hymn, is published and with John Paterson a free adaptation
       of *The Flint Heart,* Eden Phillpotts' 1910 fairy tale.

2013   I receive the Laura Ingalls Wilder Award from the American
       Library Association. *Giving Thanks,* a second book with artist
       Pamela Dalton, and *A Stubborn Sweetness,* a new collection
       of Christmas stories combining stories from the previous
       two collections with some new material, are published. John
       Paterson Sr. dies on September 30.

MY FAMILY TREE

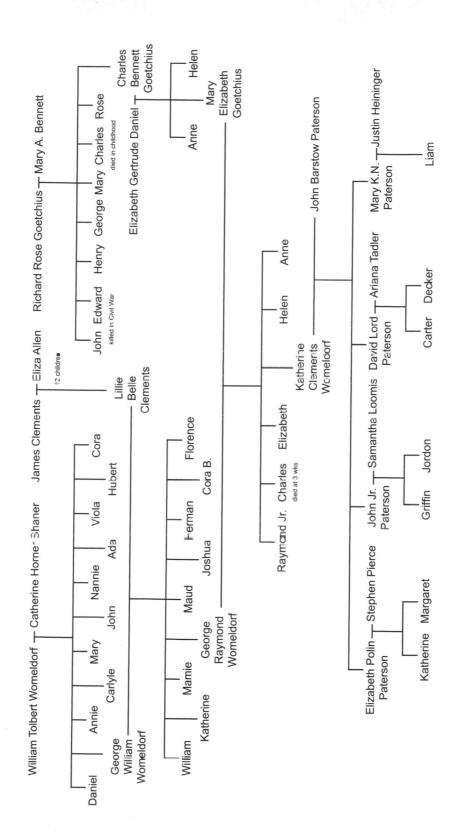